SELECTED POEMS 1956-1996

Also by Anthony Thwaite

Poems

Home Truths
The Owl in the Tree
The Stones of Emptiness
Penguin Modern Poets 18 (with A. Alvarez and Roy Fuller)
Inscriptions
New Confessions
A Portion for Foxes
Victorian Voices
Poems 1953–1983
Letter from Tokyo
Poems 1953–1988
The Dust of the World

Criticism

Twentieth-Century English Poetry
Six Centuries of Verse
Poetry Today: 1960–1995

For Children

Beyond the Inhabited World: Roman Britain

Travel and Topography

Japan (with Roloff Beny)
The Deserts of Hesperides: An Experience of Libya
In Italy (with Roloff Beny and Peter Porter)
Odyssey: Mirror of the Mediterranean (with Roloff Beny)

As Editor

Penguin Book of Japanese Verse (with Geoffrey Bownas)
The English Poets (with Peter Porter)
Larkin at Sixty
Philip Larkin: Collected Poems
Selected Letters of Philip Larkin
Selected Poems of Longfellow
Selected Poems of R. S. Thomas

ANTHONY THWAITE

Selected Poems 1956–1996

London
ENITHARMON PRESS
1997

First published in 1997
by the Enitharmon Press
36 St George's Avenue
London N7 0HD

Distributed in Europe
by Password (Books) Ltd
23 New Mount Street
Manchester M4 4DE

Distributed in the USA and Canada
by Dufour Editions Inc.
PO Box 449, Chester Springs
Pennsylvania 19425, USA

ISBN 1 900564 55 6 (paperback)
ISBN 1 900564 75 0 (hardback)
The hardback edition, bound by The Fine
Bindery, is limited to twenty-five signed
and numbered copies, each one containing
a handwritten poem from the collection.

British Library Cataloguing-in-Publication Data.
A catalogue record for this book is available
from the British Library

Set in Bembo by Bryan Williamson, Frome
and printed in Great Britain by
The Cromwell Press, Broughton Gifford, Wiltshire

Contents

'Mr Cooper–Dead'

38
The oracle, asleep
Snores in her ancient dreams
and round her head
The angels, mingling with the
harpies, weep

New Poems

for Ann

Death of a Rat

Nothing the critic said of tragedy,
Groomed for the stage and mastered into art,
Was relevant to this; yet I could see
Pity and terror mixed in equal part.
Dramatically, a farce right from the start,
Armed with a stick, a hairbrush and a broom,
Two frightened maladroits shut in one room.

Convenient symbol for a modern hell,
The long lean devil and the short squat man
No doubt in this were psychological,
Parable for the times, Hyperion
And Satyr, opposites in union . . .
Or Lawrence's *Snake*, to turn the picture round –
Man's pettiness by petty instinct bound.

But, to be honest, it was neither, and
That ninety minutes skirring in a duel
Was nothing if not honest. The demand
Moved him towards death, and me to play the fool,
Yet each in earnest. I went back to school
To con the hero's part, who, clung with sweat,
Learned where the hero, fool and coward met.

Curtain to bed and bed to corner, he
Nosed at each barrier, chattered, crouched, and then
Eluded me, till art and fear and pity
Offered him to me at the moment when
I broke his back, and smashed again, again,
Primitive, yes, exultant, yes, and knowing
His eyes were bright with some instinctive thing.

If every violent death is tragedy
And the wild animal is tragic most
When man adopts death's ingenuity,
Then this was tragic. But what each had lost
Was less and more than this, which was the ghost
Of some primeval joke, now in bad taste,
Which saw no less than war, no more than waste.

To My Unborn Child

Nothing is known but that you are
And move under her hand and mine,
Feeding and sleeping, clandestine
Agent and close conspirator.
You mould your own unique design
And grow frail roots nine months in her.

Collision of erratic spores
Moved eyes to bud, fingers to swell
Out of the light, and now he walks
On water, and is miracle.

What you will be the uncertain world
Waits for and watches, nor can make
Provision for each loose mistake
You drop when, far beyond the fold,
The days you pass, the routes you take
Teach you to be shy or bold.

The tent of flesh, the hut of bone
Shelter him on pilgrimage
And blood and water build for him
A flooded road, a shifting bridge.

Not yet real, we make for you
A toy that is reality.
The secret country where you lie
Is far from it, but no less true,
And both are dangerous to the eye
That fears what flesh and fate may do.

Tent, hut and bridge are weak as he
And yet unnumbered travellers
Have spent dark nights encamped in such
Retreats, and trod such paths as hers.

You who will soon step down through blood
To where earth, sky and air combine
To make you neither hers nor mine,
Think: you now stand where many stood
Who, each in his own unique design,
Was weak and strong and bad and good.

And yet these murmurs cannot break
The doors which you alone unbar,
And we who know all this must know
Nothing is known but that you are.

Mr Cooper

Two nights in Manchester: nothing much to do,
One of them I spent partly in a pub,
Alone, quiet, listening to people who
Didn't know me. *So I told the bloody sub-*
Manager what he could do with it. . . . Mr Payne
Covers this district – you'll have met before?
Caught short, I looked for the necessary door
And moved towards it; could hear, outside, the rain.

The usual place, with every surface smooth
To stop, I suppose, the aspirations of
The man with pencil stub and dreams of YOUTH
AGED 17. And then I saw, above
The stall, a card, a local jeweller's card
Engraved with name, JEWELLER AND WATCHMENDER
FOR FIFTY YEARS, address, telephone number.
I heard the thin rain falling in the yard.

The card was on a sort of shelf, just close
Enough to let me read this on the front.
Not, I'd have said, the sort of words to engross
Even the keenest reader, nothing to affront
The public decency of Manchester.
And yet I turned it over. On the back
Were just three words in rather smudgy black
Soft pencil: MR COOPER – DEAD. The year

Grew weakly green outside, in blackened trees,
Wet grass by statues. It was ten to ten
In March in Manchester. Now, ill at ease
And made unsure of sense and judgement when
Three words could throw me, I walked back into
The bar, where nothing much had happened since
I'd left. A man was trying to convince
Another man that somehow someone knew

Something that someone else had somehow done.
Two women sat and drank the lagers they
Were drinking when I'd gone. If anyone
Knew I was there, or had been, or might stay,
They didn't show it. *Good night*, I almost said,
Went out to find the rain had stopped, walked back
To my hotel, and felt the night, tall, black,
Above tall roofs. And Mr Cooper dead.

Night Thoughts

Darker than eyes shut in a darkened room,
Colder than coldest hours before the dawn,
My nightmare body leaves its bed to walk
Across the unseen lawn
Where apples nudge my feet. They force a shout
Inside my throat which, struggling, can't get out.

I am awake. The dream is over now.
No one is in the garden, nor has been.
You lie beside me while I count the things
Tomorrow will begin
In idleness, omission or false choice,
In lack of purpose or uncertain voice.

You sleep, and in the dark I hear you breathe
Through certainties, responsibilities.
Sometimes you tell me of your own strange dreams.
Mine are banalities,
Trudging down trodden paths to find a heap
Of fragments unromanticized by sleep.

Letters unwritten: papers on my desk:
Money: my age: things I would not have said
Given another minute to decide.
I stifle in my bed,
Searching for other names to call it by,
This blankness which comes down so finally.

But names are nothing, dreams are nothing, when
The day unrolls itself from second sleep.
Reluctantly, I wake: shave: choose a tie.
These daily things are cheap,
The small wage paid to keep my nightmares small:
Trivial, dull: not terrible at all.

At Birth

Come from a distant country,
Bundle of flesh, of blood,
Demanding painful entry,
Expecting little good:
There is no going back
Among those thickets where
Both night and day are black
And blood's the same as air.

Strangely you come to meet us,
Stained, mottled, as if dead:
You bridge the dark hiatus
Through which your body slid
Across a span of muscle,
A breadth my hand can span.
The gorged and brimming vessel
Flows over, and is man.

Dear daughter, as I watched you
Come crumpled from the womb,
And sweating hands had fetched you
Into this world, the room
Opened before your coming
Like water struck from rocks
And echoed with your crying
Your living paradox.

White Snow

'White snow,' my daughter says, and sees
For the first time the lawn, the trees,
Loaded with this superfluous stuff.
Two words suffice to make facts sure
To her, whose mental furniture
Needs only words to say enough.

Perhaps by next year she'll forget
What she today saw delicate
On every blade of grass and stone;
Yet will she recognize those two
Syllables, and see them through
Eyes which remain when snow has gone?

Season by season, she will learn
The names when seeds sprout, leaves turn,
And every change is commonplace.
She will bear snowfalls in the mind,
Know wretchedness of rain and wind,
With the same eyes in a different face.

My wish for her, who held by me
Looks out now on this mystery
Which she has solved with words of mine,
Is that she may learn to know
That in her words for the white snow
Change and permanence combine –
The snow melted, the trees green,
Sure words for hurts not suffered yet, nor seen.

Hedgehog

Twitching the leaves just where the drainpipe clogs
In ivy leaves and mud, a purposeful
Creature about its business. Dogs
Fear his stiff seriousness. He chews away

At beetles, worms, slugs, frogs. Can kill a hen
With one snap of his jaws, can taunt a snake
To death on muscled spines. Old countrymen
Tell tales of hedgehogs sucking a cow dry.

But this one, cramped by houses, fences, walls,
Must have slept here all winter in that heap
Of compost, or have inched by intervals
Through tidy gardens to this ivy bed.

And here, dim-eyed, but ears so sensitive
A voice within the house can make him freeze,
He scuffs the edge of danger: yet can live
Happily in our nights and absences.

A country creature, wary, quiet and shrewd,
He takes the milk we give him, when we're gone.
At night, our slamming voices must seem crude
To one who sits and waits for silences.

At Dunwich

Fifteen churches lie here
Under the North Sea;
Forty-five years ago
The last went down the cliff.
You can see, at low tide,
A mound of masonry
Chewed like a damp bun.

In the village now (if you call
Dunwich a village now,
With a handful of houses, one street,
And a shack for Tizer and tea)
You can ask an old man
To show you the stuff they've found
On the beach when there's been a storm:

Knife-blades, buckles and rings,
Enough coins to fill an old sock,
Badges that men wore
When they'd been on pilgrimage,
Armfuls of broken pots.
People cut bread, paid cash,
Buttoned up against the cold.

Fifteen churches, and men
In thousands working at looms,
And wives brewing up stews
In great grey cooking pots.
I put out a hand and pull
A sherd from the cliff's jaws.
The sand trickles, then falls.

Nettles grow on the cliffs
In clumps as high as a house.
The houses have gone away.
Stand and look at the sea
Eating the land as it walks
Steadily treading the tops
Of fifteen churches' spires.

Lesson

In the big stockyards, where pigs, cows, and sheep
Stumble towards the steady punch that beats
All sense out of a body with one blow,
Certain old beasts are trained to lead the rest
And where they go the young ones meekly go.

Week after week these veterans show the way,
Then, turned back just in time, are led themselves
Back to the pens where their initiates wait.
The young must cram all knowledge in one day,
But the old who lead live on and educate.

Dust

Beautiful only when the light catches it
Arrested yet volatile in a shaft of sun,
Or under the microscope, like an ancient detritus
Of snowflakes: otherwise valueless debris.
The ash from my cigarette, the air from my lungs,
The soles of my shoes, the palms of my hands, breed it,
Absorb it, carry it, disperse it. The liquids of bodies
Dry to it in the end, and the sea's salt.

Created from the beginning, it carries its beginnings
Even to the end. Metals and minerals
Are crushed to its substance: in the desert
It is beyond the harshness of sand. Soft,
Disposable, it collects in corners, to be moved
Only to another place: it cannot be moved
Finally. Indestructible, even in fire
It shapes its own phoenix, and rises with the wind.

Each second shifts it, animates its grey
Weight, bearing down on pliant surfaces.
Analyse its origins, and you find the full range
Of everything living and dead. It obeys water,
Lying down to a drenching, but as the sun
Parches that adversary it re-forms and spreads
Further and further, to the eyes, the nostrils, the throat,
A thin dry rain, contemptible, persistent.

In a world of definable objects, each different from each,
It unites as denominator of all,
The common agent. I see the white page
Gathering its random calligraphy under my pen,
And see at the tip of the pen the fine motes swirl
Down to that point where a fragmented earth
Silently whirls in an air choked with nothing but dust:
The pulverization of planets, the universe dust.

Buzzards Above Cyrene

Alone or in wheeling squadrons of dozens, they move
High above the escarpment, drift to the plain below,
The sun with a certain light obscuring their wings
So that they vanish to narrowed points of darkness
Only to swing away a moment later
Becoming spread sails, gold, brown, distinct and huge
Over tombs, junipers, red stones, red dust
Caught in a still and windless stretch of blue.
But more than that, they impose a scale by which
You measure these golden ruins, these hanging gardens of fossils,
These clear imperial edicts and pieties
Cluttering the ledges with magnificence,
All narrowed to points of light in an unwinking eye
For which, fathoms down, a mouse freezes still, a lizard
Flashes, a dung beetle labours through dry thorns,
Regarded, moved over like a dowser's twig,
To twitch then, jerk down, pounce, finding nothing there
But these poor small spoils, these puny snacks and beakfuls
Littered among ruins, squalid among remains,
Ravaged, scavenged, picked clean among pink blooms.

Arabic Script

Like a spider through ink, someone says, mocking: see it
Blurred on the news-sheets or in neon lights
And it suggests an infinitely plastic, feminine
Syllabary, all the diacritical dots and dashes
Swimming together like a shoal of minnows,
Purposive yet wayward, a wavering measure
Danced over meaning, obscuring vowels and breath.
But at Sidi Kreibish, among the tombs,
Where skulls lodge in the cactus roots,
The pink claws breaking headstone, cornerstone,
Each fleshy tip thrusting to reach the light,
Each spine a hispid needle, you see the stern
Edge of the language, Kufic, like a scimitar
Curved in a lash, a flash of consonants
Such as swung out of Medina that day
On the long flog west, across ruins and flaccid colonials,
A swirl of black flags, white crescents, a language of swords.

Ali Ben Shufti

You want coins? Roman? Greek? Nice vase? Head of god,
    goddess?
Look, shufti here, very cheap. Two piastres? You joke.

I poke among fallen stones, molehills, the spoil
Left by the archaeologists and carelessly sieved.
I am not above ferreting out a small piece
From the foreman's basket when his back is turned.
One or two of my choicer things were acquired
During what the museum labels 'the disturbances
Of 1941'; you may call it loot,
But I keep no records of who my vendors were –
Goatherds, Johnnies in berets, Neapolitan conscripts
Hot foot out of trouble, dropping a keepsake or two.
I know a good thing. I keep a quiet ear open when
The college bodysnatchers arrive from Chicago,
Florence, Oxford, discussing periods
And measuring everything. I've even done business with
    them:
You will find my anonymous presence in the excavation
    reports
When you get to 'Finds Locally Purchased'. Without a B.A. –
And unable to read or write – I can date and price
Any of this rubbish. Here, from my droll pantaloons
That sag in the seat, amusing you no end,
I fetch out Tanagra heads, blue Roman beads,
A Greek lamp, bronze from Byzantium,
A silver stater faced with the head of Zeus.
I know three dozen words of English, enough French
To settle a purchase, and enough Italian
To convince the austere *dottore* he's made a bargain.
As for the past, it means nothing to me but this:
A time when things were made to keep me alive.
You are the ones who go on about it: I survive
By scratching it out with my fingers. I make you laugh
By being obsequious, roguish, battered, in fact
What you like to think of as a typical Arab.
Well, Amr Ibn el-As passed this way
Some thirteen hundred years ago, and we stayed.

I pick over what he didn't smash, and you
Pay for the leavings. That is enough for me.
You take them away and put them on your shelves
And for fifty piastres I give you a past to belong to.

The Letters of Synesius

Synesius of Cyrene: born in Libya *c.* A.D. 370, died there *c.* A.D. 413.
Greek by ancestry, Roman by citizenship, he considered himself to be
a Libyan, a citizen of the Libyan Pentapolis, of which Cyrene, his
birthplace, was one city, and Ptolemais, of which he became bishop,
was another. He studied under Hypatia at Alexandria, visited Athens,
went as ambassador of the Pentapolis to Constantinople, and probably
died at the hands of a native Libyan tribe, the Austuriani.

*It seemed to me that I was some other person, and that I was one listening to
myself amongst others who were present . . .*

SYNESIUS to HYPATIA

LETTER I

*You must know my way of speaking the truth bluntly has
followed me even to the bounds of Libya.*

At Tocra

The ephebes set hammer and chisel to the wall
Each in his different way, with different skills.
Well-oiled conscripts, glistening and drunk,
Inscribe their achievements and their names and die.
The dragon inherits the Hesperidean gardens
And spawns small lizards, quicksilver on white rock.
Lethe has lights. The dark pools breed white fish
Nevertheless, and blind white crayfish.

Ask for the key

At the Military Academy where the Dean has just finished
Lecturing on the psychology of war.
The Jews have sacked Cyrene. In the tombs
Families sit round brewing tea.

Necropolis.

The Parliament building is locked. The wells are locked
At Gasr Lebia, where Justinian's queen
Is celebrated in mosaic: bull,
Fish, amphibious monster with a conch,
An eagle preying on a calf, crab's claws,
And perched on a curiously humped crocodile

25

A duck.
                The wells are dry, the drillers cry for oil
And find dry holes. Concession 65
Spouts oil and blood. Great wonders come to pass.
                                        The linguists say
The Berber cannot write but has an alphabet
No one can read. Tenders are asked
For a new road to Chad.
                        Somewhere between
Brega and Zelten, in a waste of sand,
A signpost on an oil-drum indicates
GIALO across the trackless distances.

The king is old. Undergraduates
Are taught philosophy by Egyptians now.
And at Tocra a boy indicates with gestures
How wide is Gamal Nasser's world. That face
Looks down as often as the king's, and smiles
Where the old man's is fatherly but stern.

Aristippus emigrated. There was visa trouble.
A cloud of dust in the east presages war
And the coming of the goat. Pink and yellow,
The posters proclaim in fancy Gothic script
'No word pease whill illeagal Isreil exists'
And 'Palesting was not Belfor's land to promise'
(Belfor the idolatrous, Baal the Ingilizi hound).

                        The ephebes have trouble
In mastering the Christian calendar,
The Latin alphabet. Teach us, they cry,
And go on strike. For the Franks, the wine is cheap
But when you walk the beach at the city's edge
The smashed Heineken bottles shine like grass:
Expensive mosaic. The earliest city lies here
Under this pile of donkeys' hooves. Dig here.
You find loom-weights from looms whose cloth has meshed
Into the sand, the salt, the lips of fossils.

I write between spells of guard between the watchtowers,
Or lecture on the English question-tag.

26

LETTER II

We have planted our fields for the fires lit by our enemies.

We have had wise men. Where are they now? we ask.
Aristippus, who taught that pleasure was highest good,
Callimachus, writing verses in his catalogue,
And, without false modesty, myself –
Synesius, mounting guard in my bishop's cope
And watching the setting sun run creases down
The great swathe of the Jebel.
                                                    I have seen
The Italian farmhouses house sheep and straw,
And vv IL DUCE flake from the pink walls,
Catching the last rays of the crumbling sun.
The fourth shore's harbours clog and choke with sand.

Severus the African, speaking slow Latin
With a Berberish accent, went on campaign.
Brute tribes were pacified, our cities flourished,
But the taxes rose, the coinage was debased
So that small coins are like water in the hand.
Our emperor died on the northern frontier
And so, in time, we turn to the east.
                                                    What stays
Is here, where some potter from Byzantium
Has pressed on the pot's foot his full-fleshed thumb.

The language with the unpronounceable sound
Made somewhere below the glottis inherits our tongue.
'Poets are followed by none save erring men,'
Said the Prophet, echoing Plato into the cave.

The ghaffir in his blanket under the stairs
Who prays five times a day to Allah the Good
Collects our garbage, has trachoma in one eye,
And shall assuredly inherit the Kingdom.

LETTER III

I would rather live a stranger among strangers.

The slopes below the cave are thick with flints.
Here they kept ammunition in the war,
And now tether a bullock to a post
Under the eaves of rock.
                              Places of the mind only,
Unvisited oases, tracks marked
On unreliable maps by engineers
Who saw the landscape from two thousand feet.

So it might be a god would wander
Over the landscape deserted by his people,
Looking for evidence that once they loved him.
Now they are gone. Delicate microliths
Like snowflakes litter the dry slopes, among thorns.

I am writing to you to talk about emptiness
Because this is empty country, 'where ruins flourish'.

At first you are frightened of dogs, their distant barks
Coming closer across the strewn, ungrateful rock,
And perhaps you pick up stones to shy them away.
You are right, you trespass. Take tea with them, learn the words
For 'please' and 'thank you', bark in Arabic,
Or whatever language is current at the time:
Try Berber, Greek, Latin, Turkish, Italian,
Compounds of these, gibbering dialects –
You will still sweat with fear, ducking down for stones
Which, it may be, are tools fashioned by men
Without a language.
                              To call a man a dog
Is an insult in many languages, but not to dogs.
They sniff the high octane at Benina as the planes take off,
Watching the passengers who have an hour
Between London and Nairobi, the pale transients.

Their yellow fur bristles, they yawn and snap.
At Hagfet er Rejma they patrol the tents,
Watching me glean the slopes for polished flakes.
My pockets are full, my hands are empty.
Look, dogs, how empty. This landscape is yours, not mine.

LETTER IV

Such are our celebrations, seasonable and of old tradition,
the good things of the poor.

Simon of Cyrene carried the cross. No Libyan
In collar and tie will carry anything.
'A proud people,' says the handout wearily,
Explaining nothing.
                Lake Tritonis, place
Of Pallas Athene's birth, dries to a salt-pan
Where tin huts void their sewage. Erytheia,
Arethusa, Aegle, Hestia, are ghaffirs:
Their sweet songs are transistorized, relayed
From Radio Cairo across miles of sand.

A donkey and a microbus collide.
The donkey limps off, noisily urinates
By the side of the road, while the bus, crumpled like paper,
Waits for repairs and insurance policies.
The old survives by demanding nothing: the new
Frets in its expectations.
                I am supposed
To lead my flock through darkness until such time
As the Kingdom descends, there is no more call for martyrs,
And the meek inherit the earth. In the new order
My people go hungry thus to cleanse themselves.

In the month of Ramadan the rain begins
This year. It is December, and the stars
Wane above grey clouds, are obscured by them.
The sea is coldly feverish. Lightning streaks
The yellow stucco and the shuttered rooms.

The honey-casks, the oil-jars and the wine
Lie at the wharf. No one puts out to sea.

What can cure the soul? What food can nourish it?
Fasting by day, they feast by night and cram
Sin down their gullets. In the church beyond the wall
The heretics draw lots for martyrdom.
I have nothing more to say of the good life,
Except – having seen so much – that to suppose
Things better rather than different is a way
Of dying only, swivelled to the past.
It is easy for me to act the Jeremiah,
To juxtapose the anomalous, debased present
With the golden fragments of a golden age.
The indigenous survives: the donkey limps off unhurt.
The silphium plants wilt in the private gardens
Since men no more expect a panacea.

Those who are to come will call our Lord a prophet
Mistaken among prophets. Spiritual pride
Gives way to pride of status, money, dress.
Unearth a marble goddess and you find
Her groin defiled with soldiers' filthiness.
The Temple of Zeus is smashed, the figurines
Pulped into lime. Farzúgha's church protects
A tribe of bats and owls. At Tansollúk
The arch is crammed with masonry and sand.

In the garrison chapel we sing 'God Save the Queen':
A proud people, enjoined to pray each week
For her and Johnson too.
                              Out of the sand
A scorpion heaves its fiery shoulders, smashed
By the spade, heavy with fire and venom. The old
Survives by demanding nothing: the new
Frets in its expectations. Simon bowed
Under the weight, the jeers. Something survives
As Ramadan and Christmas coincide
And we have little left to share but pride.

30

LETTER V

And who shall collect fruit from the desert?

The sea licks the shore with sly assurance
Where freestone masonry tumbles in pools.
Salt will never be worm-eaten, says the proverb:
It is the eater and preserver, fixed
Like mould on the surfaces of sherds, the fabric
Coins wrap themselves in, a sharp-tongued mineral,
The taste of thirst, the desert's brother, the sea's self.

I wait for something. The facile have a saying:
If life is hard on you, dwell in cities.
Watching the sea is a lifetime's occupation,
Empty of incident: looking inland
I see not emptiness but desolation.
The cities are fallen, Barca is forked with fire,
Ashes drift down on Tocra, Cyrene lies open
Like an enormous cave laid out for looting.
Here on the other side we have the sea
Rubbing and prying and investigating,
A faceless element, unharvested.

Cretans fish sponges: red mullet fills our plates
But we do not catch them. Red earth holds spilth of seeds
But we grow little, garner less. We have a mineral
More powerful than salt, liquid as sea,
Deep in its cave for looting, to sustain us.
Why should our old men sow, our young men reap?
The tall earth-delvers feed us royalties,
Our government takes tithes. Consider Esso:
It sows not, neither does it reap. Yet was ever
Woman arrayed like this one, in the Modern
Grocery Store, trousered, in high heels? In the desert
Her man plucks golden fruit, Hesperidean
Apples whose juice flows richly to the sea
To be drunk by silver tankers.

                              Undergraduates, you
Who sit your final examinations, consider
Omar Mukhtar, old man on a horse,
Who died on the gallows tortured by his wounds.
'He would have been a ghaffir now,' said one
Keen student with a sneer.
                              Omar rests now,
Thirty-three years after his death, his tomb
Built like a pink carbuncle at the edge
Of Bereniké, Euhesperides,
Benghazi – cities beckoning the wise ones
Who once found life hard, who have claimed their inheritance
Out of the salt desert, the desert, the rock,
Preserver of fallen cities, of flesh, and of oil.

LETTER VI

*Shut up here in our houses, then, as in a prison, we were to
our regret condemned to keep this long silence.*

This autumn I felt the cold in my bones when
In the fountain of Apollo the frogs were spawning.
Persephone was faceless. Above the Jebel
The thunder grumbled.

Fortune was elsewhere, ministering her mercies,
Dispensing luck to barbarians and atheists.
We on the coast repaired the aqueducts
But the water failed us.

Then winter came and the highways flooded,
Keeping us chained to our useless harbours,
Pent in by storms, letting our cattle
Wander uncared for.

Somewhere in the east the administrators filed us
Under a pile of disregarded papers.
We were forgotten, except by the hungry
Collector of taxes.

32

The Governor sends me a gilt-edged invitation
To celebrate the fourteenth year of independence.
There I shall see the outlandish consuls-general
Talking dog-Latin.

My cultivated friend, please try to send me
Whatever new books the sophists have published:
I have read the reviews in the six-month-old journals
And feel a provincial.

'We traded in shrouds: people stopped dying.'
Fortune frustrates even our death-wish.
The infant mortality figures were lost by
The census department.

Remember me now to my old friends and colleagues,
Discussing the Trinity and aureate diction:
Think of me here, awaiting the fires of
The Austuriani.

See where they squat behind the escarpment,
Ignorant of metre, of faction and schism,
Destined by favourless Fortune to be the true
Heirs of the Kingdom.

LETTER VII

*I am breathing an air tainted by the decay of dead bodies. I am
waiting to undergo myself the same lot that has befallen so many others.*

Lethe, rock fissure, dark water, warm
Breath of white mist on drifting scum, not moving
Unless a white shape moves from rock to rock.
Nostrils drink steam, the air has shapes, can be touched,
Assumes phantoms. Drink here, drink, the brackish taste
On the roof of the mouth, closed with a green coin.
I am ready to descend, to enter the cave's mouth,
To put on the mist's habit, boarding the frail
Craft that has come to claim me.

In 1938

The Lido at Lethe was opened to the public
And a poem by d'Annunzio was unveiled
Limned on a carefully ruined stele. Balbo
Offered full citizenship to all who filled in
The necessary forms. Electric cables
Illuminated the forgetful waters and
Two wrought-iron gates guarded oblivion.
Bertolo Giannoni at about this time
Managed to reach the grotto's far wall
And scratched his name in letters a metre high.
Perhaps by some irony he was one of those
Crushed by the tank-tracks of Keith Douglas's troop
On the way through to Agheila and Tripoli.
Bertolo survives on the wall, having drunk the waters.

The filth of pigeons, two fig trees' silver leaves,
Roots splayed from rock channels. Persephone in fossils.
He threw the switch and the sixty-watt bulbs flashed on
Too feebly to desecrate the pre-electric dark.
I walked on duck-boards over the breathing lake.
The mist came walking towards me.
                                        Death is a mystery
Not needing these adventitious theatricals.
In the ancient darkness the eirenic shades sleep,
Forgetting Lethe, rock fissure, dark water, warm breath.

LETTER VIII

*A camel with the mange, says the proverb, can shoulder the
burden of many asses.*

When they came to ask me to serve
We were sitting over a dish of olives, drinking
Wine from Messa, the kind that tastes of stone.
We had been talking of Constantinople, the embassy
I relished so little, so far away from home.
And then they arrived, with their wallets of documents,
Their letters and seals stowed carefully away,
Their talk of Theophilus and the weather, nervously
Waiting their chance to snare me into God's acre

Before my due time. *Divine conspiracy*,
Somebody might have called it; but *duty*
Was the burden of their discourse, that
And those filial bonds they well knew bound me
To this Pentapolis, this Libya.
                          In this land
No evangelist angled for souls, no missionaries
Humped bibles along the trade routes. The sick
Children are treated by the Adventists,
The Orthodox are visited by one priest
Whose tinny bell pierces the muezzin's cry,
The quiet white nuns herd schoolgirls here and there,
And over the dust and potholes of the town
The double-breasted cathedral sits like a presence:
Mae West or Bardot, depending on your age.
The Anglicans have 'Newmarket'
Among the officers', and their ladies', horses:
The National Anthem, punkahs from Poona, words
Hallowed in Gloucestershire and Ulster, and
Hymns of the rousing sort by Wesley and Lyte.
In this whole land there is not one Christian
With a Libyan passport.
                          So I reluctantly
Accepted what they offered: Bishop, with power
Over five crumbling cities, fortress-farms,
Immitigable desert. And they accepted
My wife ('better to marry than to burn'),
My doubts, my flinching from the sweat and blood
Of trinitarian dogma. Thus I stand,
Flawed but chosen, bewildered by that choice,
Uncertain of creed, fouled in a Marian web,
Deafened by Alexandrian echoes, armed
With episcopal power in a parish of termites.
                          Look,
At Birsis, among the rotten byres, a vaulted
Church in ruins, where a man hoes red
Soil fed with Roman water. In the rubble
A fragment shows, in frayed Greek letters, words
To the Lord, and something else I cannot read.
The servants of the Lord. Alone, he hoes and sings,
Singing to himself. Perhaps to someone else.

LETTER IX

Brought up outside the pale of the Church, and having
received an alien training, I grasped at the altars of God.

The Dalmatians have landed their advance party
And the billeting-officer is hard at work.
I can now administer the Mass in Serbo-Croat
But the congregation is thin. I carry Christ
Like a burden on my tongue. Andronicus –
From tunny fisher's perch to governor's chariot –
Is excommunicated, but runs giddy still.
My bow sprouts mould in the yard, I have given away
My dogs, my saddle.
                    Once there was philosophy
But how can that clear stream run when I spend my days
Adjudicating ruridecanal tiffs at Hydrax or Darnis,
Squabbles about copes or the laying on of hands?
Hypatia, remember the hush in the lecture-room
When you entered serenely with your astrolabe
And began to enunciate truths?
                            Tonight at five
A conversation-lesson with the Praetor, whose Greek
Would not fill a sardine. Yes, I am peevish.
You may say it is the climate or the place or my time of life –
But I carry a burden that was given to me
Which I do not understand. Somewhere, God's plan
Is hidden in monoliths or a wafer of bread.
His purpose obscurely works through those Slavs on the hill
As I offer his flesh and blood. Neither Gentile nor Jew
In that Kingdom. So I puzzle it out, till I hear
A knock at my study door. Come in, Praetor, come.

Letter X

And yet this is nothing but what the ancient oracle announced
as to how the Pentapolis must end.

What the oracle said was vapour swathing the rock,
And we could discern a finger writing in steam
As on a tiled wall the obscene words
Doing death to life in hints and half-promises.
'Libya shall perish by the wickedness of its leaders.'
Unequivocal, you think, for the oracle?
The ambiguities are all ours –
Rumours of referendum, of abdication:
Denials of rumours, official circumlocutions:
Whispers in cafés, public demonstrations,
Restoration of order, and if necessary
The 2 a.m. visits, the executions.
I hear the same story twice, and pass on
A third version, atomized by now
To fragments with different names and places,
But still – substantially, you say – but still
The truth holds, and the whisperers hold to it.
The oracle grins like a toad, and belches fumes.

Battus stammered and lisped. Coming to ask for a voice,
He was bidden instead to build an empire. Oracle,
You are the echo of ignorance, though I believe you.
For 'abounding in fleeces' read 'running over with oil'.

Conspicuous waste, money's confederate,
Marks the economy's frontiers. Tin cans,
Bottles, bones, blood, uncollected
In a city without dustbins, demonstrate
How well we are doing.
                              The cities of the plain
Flourished as we do, but a belly-dancer
At the Riviera or the Berenice
Will hardly call God down with his dust and ashes.
Dust and ashes are what is native here,
Unprophesied and sempiternal. Doom
Carries a drilling-rig in a Landrover,
A geologist from Yale, and a cloud of rumour

Stinking along the salt-pans whose flamingoes
Have flown away, over whose white plateaux
The ghibli blows from the south, bringing dust to the tongue.

Andronicus, imperialist British, wily
Egyptian agitator, Zionist, Polish agent
Disguised as an engineer — you have handed over
This traduced Kingdom. Equipped for Armageddon,
The alien cavalry rides off, but in the squares
Public loudspeakers broadcast messages
Of peace, stability, spontaneous joy,
Showing how once again etcetera
And how etcetera the future is
If only we hold firm. Etcetera.

The tomb of Battus, long located here,
In fact is there. No matter. He is dead.
The archaeologists can shift him as they please.
Fires, watchtowers, fires. The oracle, asleep,
Snores in her ancient dreams, and round her head
The angels, mingling with the harpies, weep.

LETTER XI

> *War and famine have not yet annihilated it completely, as*
> *was foredoomed; but they are wearing it away and destroying*
> *it little by little.*

Holes in the earth, places of snakes and fleas:
We shall creep in on our bellies, we shall find refuge
Among the ignorant, the outcast, those who merit
No conquest, being too low already.
There, I suppose, we shall die.
                              This 'resurrection'
I take as allegory, for when we die
There, in a hole like a brood of field-mice, can you
Imagine our suffocated, wasted bodies
Assuming, in some flash of lightning, wings
To make us rise, harps to be struck for joy,
And crowns to inherit the Kingdom? The Kingdom is here.

38

Or here, where the woman near Sirte smiles,
Smiling with stained teeth, hands red with henna,
Holding a child whose nose is running and whose ears
Are pierced for ear-rings big as saucers.
So she smiles, accustomed, poor, expecting no change.

Long before dawn the cocks are crowing here:
Their catalogue of betrayal fills the night.
At six the sky is a dome of brilliant blue,
Only at the edges furred with a grey mist
Presaging another day of burning. Who will burn?
We are not martyrs yet, and if we are
We shall not burn but be trapped in our fastnesses,
Beyond the episcopal court, the Rood, the Grail.

Hesychius, I have seen your house, its dutiful mosaics
(Where you recorded your family and our God)
Erupting like waves from centuries of rain,
Seismic disturbance, tumult of war and anthill.
The long attrition begins, the mills of God
Grind us to dust the ghibli blusters north
Into the sea where no fleet aims to fan
With Dorian sails our northward passage home.
The woman near Sirte smiles, who is to come
After barbarians, pillage, drought; and we
Are dust in the holes of the earth and under the sea.

LETTER XII

> *I am a minister of God, and perchance I must complete my
> service by offering up my life. God will not in any case overlook
> the altar, bloodless, though stained by the blood of a priest.*

I have reached the end. I shall write to you no more.
Dies irae is come. See the hole in heaven
The tribesmen of Cyrene showed to Battus.
I cling to the church's pillars. These are the Kingdom's last days.
Here are the stoups of holy water, here
The table of sacrifice. The victim is also here.

Set sail for Jedda or Jerusalem,
The miracles are due. Here is a splinter
They say is from the Rood, and here a flag
That has snuffed the air of Mecca. I leave myself
As an unholy relic, to be the dust
Neglected by the seller of souvenirs
Among his lamps, his bronzes, his rubbed coins.
Here by the shore God's altar is made whole,
Unvisited by celebrants, to be restored
By the Department of Antiquities.
Functional concrete (ruddled, grey, and brash)
Marks out what's lacking: marble, granite, wood,
The divine interstices.
                              I abdicate
Having survived locust, earthquake, death
Of children, failure of crops, murrain of hopes,
And am become that ambassador in bonds
Paul spoke of.
                    Now the muezzin calls his first
Exhortation, and the pillars fall.
Darkness is on the Jebel, tongues of flame
Bring ruin, not revelation. See how they lick
The rod of Aaron, Zelten's oily fires
Flaring against the night. The visions come.
The pilgrims have boarded, the pagans are at my throat.
The blood of a Greek is spilt for the blood of a Jew.
Altars are stained, a lamb is dragged by its legs
To bleed at the door of the house.
                                          Libya,
Image of desolation, the sun's province,
Compound of dust and wind, unmapped acres –
This is the place where Africa begins,
And thus the unknown, vaguer than my conjectures
Of transubstantiation, Trinity,
All those arcana for which, now, I die.

Monologue in the Valley of the Kings

I have hidden something in the inner chamber
And sealed the lid of the sarcophagus
And levered a granite boulder against the door
And the debris has covered it so perfectly
That though you walk over it daily you never suspect.

Every day you sweat down that shaft, seeing on the walls
The paintings that convince you I am at home, living there.
But that is a blind alley, a false entrance
Flanked by a room with a few bits of junk
Nicely displayed, conventionally chosen.
The throne is quaint but commonplace, the jewels inferior,
The decorated panels not of the best period,
Though enough is there to satisfy curators.

But the inner chamber enshrines the true essence.
Do not be disappointed when I tell you
You will never find it: the authentic phoenix in gold,
The muslin soaked in herbs from recipes
No one remembers, the intricate ornaments,
And above all the copious literatures inscribed
On ivory and papyrus, the distilled wisdom
Of priests, physicians, poets and gods,
Ensuring my immortality. Though even if you found them
You would look in vain for the key, since all are in cipher
And the key is in my skull.

The key is in my skull. If you found your way
Into this chamber, you would find this last:
My skull. But first you would have to search the others,
My kinsfolk neatly parcelled, twenty-seven of them
Disintegrating in their various ways.
A woman from whose face the spices have pushed away
The delicate flaking skin: a man whose body
Seems dipped in clotted black tar, his head detached:
A hand broken through the cerements, protesting:
Mouths in rigid grins or soundless screams –
A catalogue of declensions.

41

How, then, do I survive? Gagged in my winding cloths,
The four brown roses withered on my chest
Leaving a purple stain, how am I different
In transcending these little circumstances?
Supposing that with uncustomary skill
You penetrated the chamber, granite, seals,
Dragged out the treasure gloatingly, distinguished
My twenty-seven sorry relatives,
Labelled them, swept and measured everything
Except this one sarcophagus, leaving that
Until the very end: supposing then
You lifted me out carefully under the arc-lamps,
Noting the gold fingernails, the unearthly smell
Of preservation – would you not tremble
At the thought of who this might be? So you would steady
Your hands a moment, like a man taking aim, and lift
The mask.
            But this hypothesis is absurd. I have told you already
You will never find it. Daily you walk about
Over the rubble, peer down the long shaft
That leads nowhere, make your notations, add
Another appendix to your laborious work.
When you die, decently cremated, made proper
By the Registrar of Births and Deaths, given by *The Times*
Your two-inch obituary, I shall perhaps
Have a chance to talk with you. Until then, I hear
Your footsteps over my head as I lie and think
Of what I have hidden here, perfect and safe.

At the Frontier Post: Om

Under the one step up into the hut
A toad broods by the sergeant's shabby boots.
A single light bulb, acid and unshaded,
Marks out, inside, a function of the state
As well as marking where one road has ended.

Slogans ('To be on guard is half the battle')
Assure the walls if not the occupants.
Only behind a door do I catch glimpses
Of cruder appetites: a brown thigh, supple
With bourgeois blandishments, coyly entices.

Ripped from some old *Paris Match* or *Playboy*,
This functionary's unofficial decor
Cheers me a little as I sit and wait
While name and date of birth and date of entry
Are slowly copied to a dossier sheet.

Outside, between the frontier posts, the hills
Are black, unpeopled. Hours of restlessness
Seep from the silence, silt across the road.
At last the sergeant puts away his files,
Hands me my papers. And I see the toad

Hop into darkness, neutral and unstopped,
Companion of the brown-thighed cover girl
Hidden behind the door, beyond the frontier,
Where appetite and nature are adept
At moving quietly, or at staying still.

Soldiers Plundering a Village

Down the mud road, between tall bending trees,
Men thickly move, then fan out one by one
Into the foreground. Far left, a soldier tries
Bashing a tame duck's head in with a stick,
While on a log his smeared companion
Sits idly by a heap of casual loot –
Jugs splashing over, snatched-up joints of meat.

Dead centre, a third man has spiked a fourth –
An evident civilian, with one boot
Half off, in flight, face white, lungs short of breath.
Out of a barn another soldier comes,
Gun at the ready, finding at his feet
One more old yokel, gone half mad with fear,
Tripped in his path, wild legs up in the air.

Roofs smashed, smoke rising, distant glow of fire,
A woman's thighs splayed open after rape
And lying there still: charred flecks caught in the air,
And caught for ever by a man from Antwerp
Whose style was 'crudely narrative', though 'robust',
According to this scholar, who never knew
What Pieter Snayers saw in 1632.

Worm Within

A souvenir from Sicily on the shelf:
A wooden doll carved out of some dark wood,
And crudely carved, for tourists. There it stood
Among the other stuff. Until one night,
Quietly reading to myself, I heard
It speak, or creak – a thin, persistent scratch,
Like the first scrape of a reluctant match,
Or unarticulated word
That made me look for it within myself

As if I talked to myself. But there it was,
Scratching and ticking, an erratic clock
Without a face, something as lifeless as rock
Until its own announcement that it shared
Our life with us. A woodworm, deep inside,
Drilled with its soft mouth through the pitch-stained wood
And like the owl presaging death of good,
Its beak closing as the dynasty died,
It held fear in those infinitesimal jaws.

So – to be practical – we must choose two ways:
Either to have some expert treat the thing
(Trivial, absurd, embarrassing)
Or throw it out, before the infection eats
The doors and floors away: this Trojan horse
In miniature could bring the whole house down,
I think to myself wildly, or a whole town . . .
Why do we do nothing, then, but let its course
Run, ticking, ticking, through our nights and days?

The Bonfire

Day by day, day after day, we fed it
With straw, mown grass, shavings, shaken weeds,
The huge flat leaves of umbrella plants, old spoil
Left by the builders, combustible; yet it
Coughed fitfully at the touch of a match,
Flared briefly, spat flame through a few dry seeds
Like a chain of fireworks, then slumped back to the soil
Smouldering and smoky, leaving us to watch

Only a heavy grey mantle without fire.
This glum construction seemed choked at heart,
The coils of newspaper burrowed into its hulk
Led our small flames into the middle of nowhere,
Never touching its centre, sodden with rot.
Ritual petrol sprinklings wouldn't make it start
But swerved and vanished over its squat brown bulk,
Still heavily sullen, grimly determined not

To do away with itself. A whiff of smoke
Hung over it as over a volcano.
Until one night, late, when we heard outside
A crackling roar, and saw the far field look
Like a Gehenna claiming its due dead.
The beacon beckoned, fierily aglow
With days of waiting, hiding deep inside
Its bided time, ravenous to be fed.

Entry

Died, 1778: Moses Ozier, son of a woman out of her mind,
born in the ozier ground belonging to Mr Craft.

Christened with scripture, eponymously labelled,
You lie so small and shrunken in the verger's tall
Archaic writing. Born in the low water meadows
Down the end of lawns where you would be unlikely to walk
Supposing you'd ever got that far in life, no Pharaoh's daughter
Plucked you out of the bulrushes, for this was Yorkshire
And prophets had stopped being born. Your lunatic mother
Knelt in the rushes and squirmed in her brute pain,
Delivering you up to a damp punishing world
Where the ducks were better off, and the oziers wetly rustled
Sogged down in the marshland owned by Mr Craft.

It's sense to suppose you lasted a few days
And were buried, gratis, in an unmarked hole at the edge
Of the churchyard, the verger being scrupulous
And not wanting your skinny christened bundle of bones
To lie in unhallowed ground.

                      Poor tiny Moses,
Your white face is a blank, anonymous
Like other people's babies. Almost two hundred years
Since you briefly lay by the cold and placid river,
And nothing but nineteen words as memorial.

I hear you cry in the night at the garden's dark edge.

Elsewhere

Elsewhere, the autumn wood fills with red leaves
Silently. Worm-casts spill across meadows,
Grass withers. The sun moves west, assigning cold.

Elsewhere, a magpie clacks into the trees.
A kestrel treads on air. The path is thick
With turfed-out snail-shells, and against a gate

A squirrel hangs as hostage. Elsewhere, too,
Smoke drifts across valleys, blossoms over towns
Invested by artillery. Along highways

Drivers hurry to suburbs where lawns lie
Heavy under rain, unmown. Elsewhere children
Are rawly born. And the moon inclines its light

On domes, torn posters, curfew guards. Elsewhere,
You sit on a bed while across the corridor
A scream spirals and jerks, again, again,

Then spins down fast and settles into sobs.

And no elsewhere is here, within your head
Where nothing else is born, or grows, or dies.
Nothing is like this, where the world turns in

And shapes its own alarms, noises, signs,
Its small aggressions and its longer wars,
Its withering, its death. Outside, begins

Whatever shape I choose to give it all
(Clouds ribbed with light, signals I recognize)
But you sit silent, narrowly, in a world

So light I feel it brush my cheek, and fall.

Inscriptions

Knickers Fisher has been at work again,
Using a compass point on the closet door,
But he's a miniaturist whose main concern
Is altogether different from the team
Exhibiting on the wall by the railway line:
SMASH THE STATE stands six feet high or more
In strong black paint where the track crosses the stream –
Opposites in the field of graphic design.

And in the middle scale are the stone slabs
Pecked out by masons dead these hundred years,
Gravestones along the passage to the town:
They make their claims too, with a different voice,
But still in hope and expectation. They
Exhort and yearn and stiffly mask the fears
Of men with large obsessions and small choice,
Burdened with flesh and law till judgement day.

Points

This is the arrow which I, a warrior, shot,
Lifting up the bow-end:
Let it remind those who find it
To talk of me for ever.
        KASA KANAMURA (fl. A.D. 715–33)

I

At the Yoshino Palace, in the fifth month,
Kasa Kanamura, laureate of Nara,
Anthology compiler, brocaded and pale,
Lifted the supple bow, drew breath,
Drew back the bowstring with the bamboo arrow
And smoothly let flow forth the tip of bright metal.

It lay where it fell, away from the target,
And lay as he left it.
             He, struck (like no target)
With the thought of it lying
Where it had fallen
To stay there . . . And so
'I, a warrior' flowed smooth from his brush
On the scroll before him, as he fingered the syllables
And spoke without breath
And walked to his grave,
Who had seen the quick torrents
Shouldering the mountains
And the tumbling cascades
Race by the palace
(Stout-timbered, stone-walled) and
'In dread of their majesty'
Had sunk in his mind
To the rock-bed below,
And had stood, his mind floating
Like Mitsune after him . . .
Arrow, bright arrow
Fallen, there.

II

Fluted like this one, no longer than the first joint
Of my little finger, the bright bronze burnished
Under the weathers of twelve hundred years:
And not among grave goods, with cuirass and bracelet
Or gilded helmet or suppliant vessels,
But lodged in the thick grass of a humid summer
To lie under plaited leaves, under welts of mud,
Pressed down, trodden under, lost where it landed
In a curve out of air from bow, gut, pressure
Of fingers against arc of muscle, of air . . .

III

Today is the anniversary
Of Gamae, Nasamonian, one who ate locusts
And slept in the tombs of his ancestors
So as to dream prophecies:
Today such a man died
Somewhere in the desert north of the Psylli
Who were buried as they marched
To vanquish the South Wind.

And today, too, the anniversary
Of Arx, miner of obsidian,
Who lugged the black nuggets from a cliff on Lipari
To be fashioned by other men: and of Oyu,
Carver of bone amulets in Hokkaido:
Of Tacan, acolyte, of Chichen Itza – all
Inventions, you take it rightly, type-names of the nameless
Whose artefacts are numbered, labelled, filed
In corridors, in dustless libraries,
Mapped by distribution, plotted by computer,
Under whose alluvial tonnage the nostrils drew in air
And suffocated at the mortal touch.

Humbled among trophies, mementoes not only of death.

IV

At Karnak the lintels
At Thebes the pediments
At Antioch the walls
At Nineveh the pavements
At Konarak the platforms
At Sidon the bollards
At Troy the columns
At Angkor the terraces . . .
Yoshino fallen, the thousand ages
Drawn to the point of the tip of an arrow.

V

And at Augila the dates
The salt hills gushing water
And the crying of women
And Ghirza buried:
Acreage of stones
Above wells of water
And a flake of volcano
Flashing black fire,
Worked with the thumb
Shaped into sharpness
The tooth of the serpent
Hardened to stone
The flail of the scorpion
Petrified, polished

The armature perished
The poison crushed
To crystals of dust.

VI

In the palm of my left hand
Among the unread lines
The arrowhead lies cupped:
Its point, still sharp, defines
Its purpose, its abrupt
Quiddity. To end
Function is not to kill,
Nor lack of it to die.
The thousand ages cram
Survival's narrow way
With fragments. What I am
Emerges from the rubble.

VII

A topography of debris – clay, stone, bronze –
Dry hills of Mamelukes, Ghadames slagheaps,
The tells of Troy, the tip of Aberfan,
The mounds and spills at boundaries, beyond limits,
Smoking like Golgotha
                              as the ash descends
Sealing the thrown waste, the scoured junk,
Burying the scourings, embalming the long lost.
                              No sudden blast of cobalt
In the revelations of August, the fleshprint
                              shadowed on stone
As ghost presence, instant eidolon, but
A longer dying, a protracted chapter
Of accidents and discarded product:
The slaughter of utensils, the annihilation of weapons,
Carcases of tools, scattering of stones,
Lifted into the air by the grovelling shovel, and held
Here in the obsolete point that missed the target to
'Remind those who find it
                              to talk of me forever.'

VIII

And so it does,
Though not as you meant it,
Not knowing beyond Nara
The islands and mountains
Or seeing forever
Stretch to this point. Yet
Your poem contains
Its own assurance,
A blind inheritance
We share, in going on
Because we must,
Surviving destruction,
Valuing the dust.

The Procession

And when you have waited there so patiently
And at last the great procession passes by
With those sad, slow tunes you hummed interminably,
How will you join them? Will you somehow try
To draw attention with a slogan scratched
Hurriedly on a bit of paper, sound
A trumpet from the window where you watched,
Hope that by standing by you will be found
Among the million others? None of these.
No matter how confused and large the crowd,
Or how well-disciplined and separate
Those solemn marchers, you will step with ease
Down from the jostling pavement, be allowed
To join them. And you will not hesitate.

By the Sluice

It pulses like a skin, at dusk
Is shaken like dusty silk. The current moves
But takes its impetus and gathers speed
Only beyond the sluice-gate. Here, the faint
Shudders, the morse of water almost trapped,
Perform half mesmerized, half dying too.

Yet are not dying: those trembling dots, those small
Reverberations, rise from what is hidden –
Scatters of minnows, nervous hair-triggered fry –
Grasping at sustenance, grabbing at what is given,
Submerged ferocities, brute delicacies.

What have I hidden here, or let go, lost,
With less to come than's gone, and so much gone?
Under the gate the river slams its door.

At the Indus

It was wide, true, but no wider than the straits:
Most of it boulders and pebbles, the water itself
An uneven grey-blue snake, writhing in bursts
Here and there, but elsewhere sluggish with puddles.
It was not the size of that river, or the distance they'd come,
Or the men dead with delirium, or those killed in battle,
Or the exhaustion of a long campaign. But was it
Fear of the mountains rising red from the plain,
Fear of the unknown tribes on the other side?

                                        No,
However the legends go, or the histories patch it together,
The place was not ready. Over the other side,
Whatever travellers had come in their ones and twos
Over the centuries, was a possible paradise,
Untouched, immaculate, the dreamt-of place
(Though not for those who lived there: it never is).
We hesitate at those portals, whether Greek or Jew,
Bond or free, freethinker or devout, and are quiet
When, for a moment, history comes to a stop.
The regimental commanders muttered together; the battalions rested;
The leader was informed.
The bend of the river waited, and went on waiting.
The mountains, the buzzards, the plain, and the other side
Waited. The signal was given.

Then they turned back.

Thomas

He crossed the dry ford and the rock-strewn course
Coming towards the city: Taxila.
Behind him, to the West, a slow loss
Of blood, not his, a show of open wounds
Not yet to be healed. He had come so far
Language had left him: he conversed in signs,
And heard replies in meaningless grunts, rough sounds,
Yelps and choked gutturals, as a dog that whines
Under a bully's blows.

               How could he bring the word
To aliens like these? What wordless miracle
Could his dubiety raise and reveal?
Practical skills, the trade of strain and stress,
The palpable structure planned in wood and stone –
These were his passport. He had come so far
Commissioned and professional: the king's messengers
Insisted on his foreign competence,
His smart outlandishness. A palace, wrought
Out of daedalian magnificence . . .
He passed between the city walls, alone,
Trusting his still invisible harbinger,
And found the king.

               The man who wanted proof
And touched those dripping hands, that leaking sore,
Laid out his stylus and his plans before
A king of men, and pitched the palace roof
High up in heaven, a mansion without walls,
Unprovable, unseen, where the rooftree falls
Down to its cloudy base, its starry floor.

Rescue Dig

In a fading light, working towards evening,
Knowing next day the contractors will be there,
Impatient earth-movers, time-is-money men,
And the trench, hastily dug, already crumbling
(No leisure for revetments), you're suddenly aware
Of some recalcitrant thing, as when your pen
Stubs at the page
And slips stubbornly, tripped by a grease-spot, dry
Shadow-writing. The trowel hits the edge,
Solid against solid, perhaps pottery,
Perhaps bone, something curved and flush
With earth that holds it smooth as yolk in white
And both within their shell. Feel round it, go
Teasing its edges out, not in a rush
Of treasure-hunting randomness, but quite
Firmly yet tactfully, with a patient slow
Deliberation, down
Round the bounding line that holds it, up
Its cupped outline (grey or brown?
The light is bad), letting the soil slip
Smoothly away. Too quick in your eagerness
And you'll fracture its flimsy shape, be left with scraps.
What are these folds on it? A skull's brow-ridges,
Lugs at a pot-rim? Let your hand caress
Its texture, size and mass, feel for the gaps
That may be there, the tender buried edges
Held by the earth.
Now what you want is time, more time, and light,
But both are going fast. You hold your breath
And work only by touch, nothing in sight
Except the irrelevant spots of distant stars
Poised far above your intent groping here.
Exasperated, suddenly sensing how
Absurd your concentration, your hand jars
The obstinate thing; earth falls in a damp shower;
You scrabble to save it, swearing, sweating. Now,

In the total dark,
You know it's eluded you, broken, reburied, lost,
That tomorrow the bulldozers will be back;
The thing still nameless, ageless; the chance missed.

A Portion for Foxes

Psalm 63: 10

One streaked across the road in front of us
At night – a big-brushed grey one, almost a wolf
I liked to think – somewhere in the Punjab,
Close to a village where no doubt it scavenged.
And then back home, in England,
To see what our cat brings in –
The heads of sparrows,
A mole's pink paws, the black and marbled innards
Torn from a rat, a moorhen's claws:
Rejected spoils, inedible souvenirs,
A portion for foxes.

But here there are few foxes, no wolves,
No vultures shuffling scraggily in treetops,
No buzzards drifting in sunlight, or jackal wailing
At the edge of the compound. Only a ginger cat,
Ferociously domestic, stalking the meadows
For small and lively prey, far from those borders
Where 'fall by the sword' is no Sunday metaphor
Echoed antiphonally down gentle arches,
Where even now the gleam on a raised blade
Brings back the unspeakable, the mounds of fallen
Lying in lanes, in ditches, torn, dismembered,
A sacrifice to the wrathful god, or gods:
A portion for foxes.

Marriages

How dumb before the poleaxe they sink down,
Jostled along the slaughterer's narrow way
To where he stands and smites them one by one.

And now my feet tread that congealing floor,
Encumbered with their offal and their dung,
As each is lugged away to fetch its price.

Carnivorous gourmets, fanciers of flesh,
The connoisseurs of butcher-meat – even these
Must blanch a little at such rituals:

The carcasses of marriages of friends,
Dismemberment and rending, breaking up
Limbs, sinews, joints, then plucking out the heart.

Let no man put asunder . . . Hanging there
On glistening hooks, husbands and wives are trussed:
Silent, and broken, and made separate

By hungers never known or understood,
By agencies beyond the powers they had,
By actions pumping fear into my blood.

Simple Poem

I shall make it simple so you understand.
Making it simple will make it clear for me.
When you have read it, take me by the hand
As children do, loving simplicity.

This is the simple poem I have made.
Tell me you understand. But when you do
Don't ask me in return if I have said
All that I meant, or whether it is true.

Essays in Criticism

I like this more than that.
That is better than this.
This means this and that.
That is what this one wrote.
This is not that at all.
This is no good at all.
Some prefer this to that
But frankly this is old hat.
This is what Thissites call
Inferior this, and yet
I hope I have shown you all
That that way likes a brick wall
Where even to say 'Yes, but . . . '
Confuses the this with the that.

Instead, we must ask 'What is this?'
Then, 'Is that *that* sort of this,
Or a modified this, or a miss
As good as a mile, or a style
Adopted by that for this
To demonstrate thisness to those
Who expect a that–inclined prose
Always from this one – a stock
Response from readers like these.'
But of course the whole thing's a trick
To make you place *them* among those
Who only follow their nose,
Who are caught on the this/that spike
But who think they know what they like.

A Girdle Round the Earth

'King Rear was foorish man his girls make crazy'
Says something certainly about the play.
'Prutus fall on sord for bolitical reason'
Is unambiguous, though not the way
We native-speakers might have put it, who share
A language with the undoubted global poet.
In Tokyo or Benghazi, he abides
Our questioning syllabus still, will never stay
For an answer as the candidates all stare
Into the glossaried cryptograms he hides.

O Saku Seppiya, Shakhs Bey-er, O you
Who plague the schools and universities
From Patagonia to Pakistan,
From Thailand to Taiwan, how would it please
Your universal spirit to look down
And see the turbans and burnouses bent
Above your annotated texts, or see
Simplified Tales from Lamb by slow degrees
Asphyxiate the yellow and the brown?
To pick up the quotation, 'thou art free' –

But Matthew Arnold, schools inspector, who
Saw you 'self-school'd, self-scann'd', could not have known
How distantly from Stratford and the Globe
With British Council lecturers you've flown:
Midsummer Nights in Prague and Kathmandu,
Polonius stabbed dressed in a gallabiyah,
Shylock the Palestinian refugee,
And Hamlet's father's Serbo-Croat groan,
Dunsinane transported to Peru,
Kabuki for All's Well, Noh for King Lear.

'To be or not to be. Is that a question?'
The misquotations littering the page,
The prose translations fingermarked with sweat,
You prove again, world-wide, 'not of an age
But for all time', the English Ala' ad-Din,
The Western Chikamatsu, more than both
And different from either, somehow worth
Those sun-baked hours in echoing lecture-halls,
On torn tatami or dune-drifted stage:
'Lady Macbeth is houswif full of sin',
'Prince Hel is drinkard tho of nobel berth.'

For Louis MacNeice

Your long face, like a camel's, swivels round
The long bar of the George, and stops at me
Coming in like bad news. The BBC
Recruits young graduates to rescue Sound
From all that bright-lit, show-biz sort of stuff
And I am one of them, arrived too late
For the Golden Age (the exact date
October Fifty-Seven), though enough
Remains like a penumbra of great days
To sanctify our efforts. There you stand
Aloof and quizzical, the long bar scanned
For friends or enemies, a scornful phrase
Poised to put down the parasite or bore;
But underneath that mask a lonely man
Looks out, lugubrious comedian
Or elegiac dandy, more and more
Driven into the corners of yourself.
Uncertain of your mood, after an hour
Of a shared office going slowly sour
With cigarettes and hangovers, the shelf
Above your desk capsizing with its load
Of scripts that date back sixteen years or more,
I try the Twickenham ploy, the sort of war
You relish, England-Ireland, worth an ode
Better than J.C. Squire tried long ago.
That does it. You prefer such stuff to bleak
Intensities of bookishness, and speak
With passion of who scored, and how, and know
Each quiddity of form and style and skill.
And yet I play this game only to thaw
That icy stare, because I'm still in awe
Of your most private self, that self you spill
Into the poems you keep locked away.
Looked back on now, how much I must despise
That Boswell-type with deferential eyes
Who saw you as a lion on display!
The living man eluded me. Through praise
Bitten out from those pursed, laconic lips
Astonished me, dismissal could eclipse

My universe for hours, even days.
Now that you're dead, I read you and I hear
Your nasal, almost strangled voice recite
Poems you wrote in loneliness at night,
Far from the George and parasites and beer.
My glum prosaic homage comes too late,
Ten years too late, for your embarrassment,
And yet those truant hours spent and mis-spent
Off Portland Place I humbly dedicate
To a Muse who watches, listens, is aware
Of every sell-out, every careless word,
Each compromise, each syllable that's blurred
With vanity or sloth, and whose blank stare
Chills and unmasks me as yours used to do.
Forgive me, Louis, for such well-meant verse,
Such running-on where you would have been terse,
And take the thanks I meant to give to you.

Called For

Emily's

Tonight we drive back late from talk and supper
Across miles of unlit roads, flat field and fen,
Towards home; but on the way must make a detour
And rescue you from what, half-laughingly,
We think of as your temporary world –
Some group or other, all outlandishly
Named and rigged up in fancy dress and loud
With adolescent grief. Well, we're too old
For alien caperings like that. The road
Runs towards home and habit, milk and bed.

That unborn child I locked up in neat stanzas
Survives in two or three anthologies,
An effigy sealed off from chance or changes.
Now I arrive near midnight, but too early
To claim you seventeen years afterwards:
A darkened auditorium, lit fitfully
By dizzy crimsons, pulsing and fading blues
Through which electric howls and snarled-out words
Isolate you (though only in my eyes)
Sitting among three hundred sprawling bodies.

Your pale face for a second looms up through
The jerking filters, splatterings of colour
As if spawned by the music, red and blue
Over and over – there, your face again,
Not seeing me, not seeing anything,
Distinct and separate, suddenly plain
Among so many others, strangers. Smoke
Lifts as from a winter field, obscuring
All but your face, consuming, as I look,
That child I gave protective rhetoric.

Not just this place, the tribal lights, the passive
Communion of noise and being young,
Not just the strident music which I give
No more than half an ear to; but the sense
Of drifting out into another plane
Beyond the one I move on, and moved once
To bring you into being – that is why
I falter as I call you by your name,
Claim you, as drifting up towards me now
You smile at me, ready for us to go.

At Marychurch

(Philip Henry Gosse, 1857)

Here at the bench in front of me, the flasks
Ripple and throb with all the simulacra
Providence has provided; the various tasks
Assigned to each and all by their Creator
Perform and are performed. Forests of spines,
Vitals enclosed in hollow boxes, shells
Built of a thousand pieces, glide along
Majestically over rock and reef.
Yonder a *Medusa* goes, pumping its sluggish way
Laboriously, not ineffectually,
Beneath the surface of the clear wave;
A mass of *Millepore*, a honeycomb
Much like the second stomach of an Ox,
Slimes, reappears, retires, appears once more;
And there, that massive shrub of stone, the coy
Calcareous atoms of the *Madrepore*,
Short branches, branched and branched again, pierced through
With holes innumerable, threaded with tentacles.
Ha! Here is the little architect
Ready to answer for himself; he thrusts his head
And shoulders from his chimney-top, and shouts
His cognomen of *Melicerta ringens*.
Look! He is in the very act of building
Now. Did you see him suddenly
Bow down his head and lay a brick upon
The top of the last course? And now again
He builds another brick; his mould a tiny cup
Below his chin, his sole material
The floating floccose atoms of his refuse. So
Prochronically pellets build to bricks,
Eggs from their chambers, sharks from embryos,
The hollow cones that are the present teeth
Of crocodiles, the tusks of elephants
Refined through layer after layer until
Centuries are accomplished year by year –

And then, after the pulpy fibrous doors
Knocked on in the vegetable world,
The lower tribes, the higher forms – then Man,
Our first progenitor, the primal Head.
What shall we say, we who are chyle and lymph,
Blood, lungs, nails, hair, bones, teeth, phenomena
In the condition of the skeleton
Distinct, the navel corrugated here . . . ?
I ask you this: could God have made these plants,
These animals, this creature that is Man,
Without these retrospective marks? I tell you, no!
A Tree-form without scars limned on its trunk!
A Palm without leaf-bases! Or a Bean
Without a hilum! No laminae
Upon the Tortoise plates! A Carp without
Concentric lines on scales! A Bird that lacks
Feathers! A Mammal without hairs,
Or claws, or teeth, or bones, or blood! A Foetus
With no placenta! In vain, in vain,
These pages, and these ages, if you admit
Such possibilities. That God came down
And made each each, and separately, and whole,
Is manifest in these. Let us suppose
That this, the present year, had been the special
Particular epoch in world history
God had selected as the true beginning,
At his behest, his fiat – what would be
Its state at this Creation? *What exists*
Would still appear precisely as it does.
There would be cities filled with swarms of men;
Houses half-built; castles in ruins; pictures
On artists' easels just sketched in; half-worn
Garments in wardrobes; ships upon the sea;
Marks of birds' footsteps on the mud; the sands
Whitening with skeletons; and human bodies
In burial grounds in stages of decay.
These, and all else, the past, would be found now
Because they are found in the world now, the present age,
Inseparable from the irruption, the one moment
Chosen, the constitution, the condition:
They make it what it has been, will be, is.

The flasks ripple, subside. I am tired. And miles away
I know who sits and writes and tests and proves
Quite other things and other worlds. I fix
My microscope on *Case-fly* and on *Julus*,
The field left clear and undisputed for
The single witness on this other side,
Whose testimony lies before me now:
'In Six Days God Made Heaven and Earth, the Sea,
And All That In Them Is.' Amen. Amen.

MESSAGES FROM GOVERNMENT HOUSE

(James Ramsay, Marquess of Dalhousie, 1848-56)

The Punjab war is done: in all the land
No man in arms against us. Those who bolted
Ran through the Khyber Pass and go on running.
They came like thieves and dash away like thieves.
The Maharajah and the Council signed
Submission yesterday, the British colours
Were hoisted on the Citadel of Lahore,
The Koh-i-noor surrendered to our Queen,
And the Punjab – each inch of it – proclaimed
A portion of our Empire. What I have done
Is my responsibility. I know it
Just, politic, and necessary; my conscience
Tells me the work is one I pray that God
May bless; and with tranquillity I await
My country's sanction and my Queen's approval.

It is not every day an officer
Adds to the British Empire such a prize –
Four million subjects, and the priceless jewel
Of Mogul Emperors to his Sovereign's crown.
This I have done – but do not think that I
Exult unduly: I do not. But when
I feel conviction honestly that this deed
Is for the glory of my land, the honour
Of her most noble majesty, the good

Of those whom I have brought under her rule,
Fitly I may indulge a sentiment
Of honourable pride. Glory to God
For what has been achieved.

                Some other matters:
A curious discovery at Rangoon –
Digging an old pagoda to make way
For army barracks, our men came across
Gold images and bracelets, with a scroll
Showing these things were put there by a queen
Five hundred years ago. In all such places
One or more images are found of Buddha:
Our fellows call them 'Tommies'. There are few
Pagodas to be seen without a hole
Made by ingenious Britons in their search
For Tommies. I am sorry to admit –
Accessory after the fact, you know –
I purchased secretly myself some bits
Of this mythology when first I reached
Burmah.

        I have a sad death to report –
Bold as his sword, high-minded, kindly, pure,
Devoted to his calling, Mountain is gone.
A Christian soldier, died as he lived. He rests
In the old cemetery at Futteghur.
His widow's on her way here; he'll go home
By the next steamer.

              I have just received
A packet of the rhododendron seeds
Despatched from Kooloo, which the Duchess wished,
And trust they will do well.

           The troops have driven
Moung Goung Gyee out of the Irawaddi:
They took him in the jungle – took his gong,
His gold umbrella and his wife. A pity
The man himself escaped. The place is quiet.

From Barrackpore to Simla, from Peshawar
To Kunawar and Chini, from the camp
At Umritsur to Attok, there is peace.
The reinforcements from Madras have come,
So now I calculate 14,000 men
(5,000 Europeans) are there, thirteen
Steamers upon the river, besides marines
And many sailors. Opium stands high –
On each *per mensem* sale the Government
Gains well. The punishment we meted out
To Rani and to Bunnoo is rewarded –
The Rani people whom Sir Colin thrashed
Last May, destroying valley, stoup and roup,
Have just come in with turbans in their hands
Begging forgiveness, offering allegiance,
Submitting to our fortress. Our success
In sowing dissension between tribe and tribe,
'Twixt Mussulman and Sikh, Hindoo and all,
Is clear: suspicion reigns, and union
Is hopeless between any. Peace and plenty!

★

Just as the office mail was going out,
A rising in Bengal among the hills –
Barbarous folk, though usually timid,
Armed just with bows and arrows: some say greed,
Some say fanaticism, some ill-treatment
By those who build the railway. Troops are there
And closing in. The trouble has not spread
And soon should be put down. But what vexation
Just at the close of my career . . .

★

Before I lay this sceptre down, I plan
To show the court in a most frank despatch
What has been done in India these eight years –
And left undone. I look things in the face.
'Opus exegi': taking leave of those
I ruled over, tomorrow I embark.

75

The Friend of India some months ago
Called me 'not personally popular'.
If that is true – 'tis not for me to say –
Never were full and copious tears so shed
Over a man *unpopular*, wiped away
By bearded men . . .

              I am quite done; my leg
Gives pain continually. Let Canning do
The best he can: the brightest jewel of all
In our imperial crown weighs heavily.
Less easy every day the burden lies –
Annex one province, two others will rise up
Like hydra-headed monsters, their partition
A parturition. What will be born of this?
Rumours and panics and religious wrath
At a few cartridges . . . and 'hope deferred'
At Delhi, given time, indeed one day
'Makes the heart sick' in England. Blow away
The rebels from our cannons, still there hangs
A cloud of blood above the hills and vales,
Ganges, and Indus, and my lost domains.

AFTER HIGH TABLE

(Oxford, c. 1870)

Hockley is turning Papist, so they say:
His set is stiff with incense, and he bobs
Most roguishly in chapel. More and more
The Whore of Babylon extends her sway.
Branston is fiddling with his 'little jobs',
Copying the Bursar's buttery accounts
Into a pocket book he locks away.
In Common Room each night, the floor
Is held by Foxton, face flushed like a plum
About to drop – and we have seen him drop
Drunk as a carter in the smouldering grate.

They are all here, my *Corpus Asinorum*,
Donkeys in orders, stuffed in jowl and crop.
One day it will be said 'He did the state
Some service', when they read my book of fools.

The Master's slack. He does not know the rules.
He is – can't be denied – a natural curate
And would be better suited to the cure
Of souls in Wiltshire, ministering to pigs.
I've seen old Figgins watch him like a ferret,
For Figgins was passed over, and for sure
Preferment went because Enthusiasts
Clamoured for someone without Roman views.
But – pardon me – the Master strokes and frigs
His conscience like a trollop with an itch
Flat on her back and panting in the stews.
All pious mush dressed up as manliness,
Evangelistic canting, keen to bring
Trousers to niggers who don't wear a stitch.
A man's religion is his own. To sing
Barnstorming stanzas to the Lord's as poor
As Newman fluting eunuch fancyings,
His heavenly choir on earth. O that old Whore,
How devious she becomes!

                                This elm-smoke stings
My eyes at night, when I should be holed up
Snugly behind the bulwark of my oak.
Some more Marsala, or another cup
Of punch . . . What frowsty collared priest is this,
Another chum of Kingston's on the soak
Or snivelling gaitered surrogate from Bath?
Give me your arm – I needs must go and piss.

My colleagues all tread down the primrose path
That – who? – oh, Shakespeare then – put in a play.
I should be even now, I tell you, hard
Pent in my room and working at my book,
Theocritus, my text, my elegiac
Pagan . . .

77

How these chatterers swill and stay!
I'll take a turn with you around the yard,
The farther quad where dotards never look,
Or if they do, then always back and back
To the dark backward and abysm of time . . .
But then we are all backward-lookers here,
If you would understand me: relicts, men
Who hear the echo when we hear the chime,
As Great Tom stuns the silence. In my ear
I sense the falter of the tolling bell,
I hear it boom again, again, again,
Fetching me back and back, not boding well,
And the full moon hangs high across St Ebbe's . . .

Where was I? Morbid, maybe, at this hour
When Master, Bursar, Chaplain, Dean and all
Waddle like corpulent spiders in their webs
To winding staircases and narrow beds,
To livings without life, posts without power,
A benefice without a benefit.
I have you all marked down . . .

A MESSAGE FROM HER

(Mary Ellen Meredith, 1861: Modern Love, V)

I

So I dissembled: you dissembled too,
Striving to gain the fame you could not have.
You thought me your importunate young slave.
I thought you fierce to attain the things that you,
You only, could achieve. So we were wrong
In feigning each was only bent on each,
Eyes signalling to eyes, not needing speech.
The labour hence was tortuous and long,
Words broke to sentences, each phrase strung out
Like drunken men striving to stretch their thirst
Into the dawn, or lovers who at first
Believe each touch and kiss a final bout,

And then renewed, renewed . . . And each goes on
Battling, and feinting, reeling under blows
That deaden as the deadly feeling grows
That they are dead indeed; and dead and gone.

II

That gentle painter with beseeching eyes –
He was no menace: not the first, at least.
Some other bore the sign, mark of the beast,
Before he ever came. What sad surprise
When I escaped – more matter for your art!
This was the dizzy sickening of your will,
Sisyphus labouring up the stony hill,
Something that drained the nerves and pierced the heart:
An emptiness that gave me room to breathe
But vacuum to you – and how you strove,
Your lungs protesting, with what you used to love,
Your murderess . . . So our passions seethe,
Spill over, settle, chill. We learn to die
By living our own lives, leaving a room
Furnished like any self-respecting tomb,
The funeral bands disguising vacancy.

III

I left a note: 'He is in tears – I must
Go to him now.' And so the hours went by,
And you, of course, knew I could never lie.
But there I lay, lapped in an alien lust
That you could never understand, nor ever
Satisfy. Those broodings, those inert
And silent pangs that shadowed your sad hurt,
How could you contemplate what came to sever
Mismatched endurances with such a blow?
My love – my once love – you were far away,
Remembering some distant hallowed day
When from my gown I let the loose bands go
And I was Princess to your wandering Prince,
And all was fable, Land of Faery . . .
What you cast out, what you could never see –
That was the simple truth, long vanished since.

IV

No word of me in letters, never a word
Let fall from that point onwards that I shared
Eight years with you, or that I ever cared
Concerning you. Fled like a migrant bird
To climes unknown, in ignorance I became
A footnote to your *opus*, quite cast out
Like the lean scapegoat who must bear the doubt
Because no other creature bears the blame.
And so I sickened – pitiless endless pain,
The swellings and the achings. Pale and weak,
I stumbled into debt, wrote letters, bleak
Day after day. For you, the deadly strain
Was not *my* dying but *your* distant fear
Of sickness and of death. I knew I must
Face on my own the test, accept the just
Reward for sin, and nowhere seek a tear.

V

How strange to be remembered in this way!
A set of almost-sonnets, crabbed yet rich,
Abrupt yet ample, stitch woven into stitch
As line by line you tell the present day
What happened, who kept silent, which one spoke
Words that must wound, how reverie went wrong,
And each verse carrying its bitter song –
Bitter, reproaching nothing but the yoke
That kept us bound together. This is how
Art will remember us, not in the ways
That stretched and broke us through those racking days
But in the mode that's apt and modish now:
Art for Art's sake . . . Forsaken, you set down
A set of tablets permanent as stone.
I was a wisp, a nothing, on my own,
Commemorated with an iron crown.

FROM THE VILLA MASSONI

('Ouida', 1909)

A dozen dogs, poodles and nondescripts,
My darlings barking at the iron gate . . .
Who might it me? There's no one left to call,
And so I sit useless, the garden wall
High as my disappointment, sit and wait
For the moths to eat away the innocence,
The honesty, the decency, and then
The whole new wardrobe I could not afford
From Worth — the vanity, the vain expense,
The flirting with Marchese and with Lord,
The opinionated converse with true men.

Now Robert Lytton's dead — a heart attack —
And della Stufa — cancer of the throat —
And Mario, too, whose voice enslaved me once —
All loves, all friendships, straitened and remote
As former fame, and flower-filled hotel rooms,
The Langham thirty years ago . . . Look askance,
You moralists who jib at genius,
As the pert message posted in the hall —
'Leave morals and umbrellas at the door.'
No invitation to reception, dance,
Wine, *conversazione*, concert, play,
For — what? — a dozen years . . . A villa, dank
And crumbling among cypresses, four floors,
Twenty-five rooms — myself and Gori stay
When Bagni drifts with leaves, and all have left.
Condemned to solitude, in poverty,
Furniture seized by creditors, bereft
Even of letters bundled over years,
Manuscripts auctioned, each royalty and fee
Reduced to farthings . . . No, these are not tears
But the dulled liquids of blue eyes that saw
Irving perform my gestures and my words.
Out of the world, my world, perhaps so much
The better, walled up here midst dogs and trees —
I am old, pathetic, angry, out of touch.
The world takes its revenge on us, because

We once despised it. Play it as you please,
Rewards must dwindle, style must go awry,
Voluptuousness grow vile, and Europe learn
The rage for slaughter. Middle-class spirits crush
The rapture and the passion of the soul,
Making it mute: thus Browning, Tennyson,
George Eliot – in chains, or chanting odes,
Or hypocritical in homilies.
Our genius is our spur, our passion goads
The highest from the best. Even in the tomb
The lustre shines like gold from sepulchres
Of lost Etruscan kings, or on the breast
Of some fair living woman, undimmed by dust,
The length of ages, or men's pettiness.

*

My dogs bark on among the cypress gloom,
A dozen Cerberuses whose yelps press
Hotly against the neglected effigy –
My own – where like a Florentine princess
I lie in Bagni, dead, unread, my name
A half-romantic joke, something to see
If tourists can be bothered to search out
A deaf custodian with a rusty key.
No flowers, no candles, no *frisson*-laden words
Await you there: the candles have gone out,
The flowers have faded, and the words are dull
As out-of-fashion dusty ballroom clothes
Hanging in wardrobes in deserted rooms.
The iron bell-handle's broken: when you pull,
The dogs grow hoarse not at the sound of it
But at the unfamiliar, painful smell
Which men call Life. And I am out of it.

Letter from Tokyo

This season of spring/summer/autumn/winter is treacherous.
Please be vigilant of your fragile health throughout it.

My garden is only the size of a cat's forehead.
This is because my fees are a sparrow's tears.

You are welcome to visit me whenever you wish,
Though the squalor of my abode will shock your feet.

Your handsome frame undoubtedly will suffer
From submitting to the rabbit-hutch I inhabit.

Perhaps when spring/summer/autumn/winter succeed in their courses
I may trouble you with another communication.

My command of your language is, you will see, defective.
Can you understand my poor meaning? That is remarkable.

Cicadas in Japan

Hearn heard them, and thought them magical,
Tried to distinguish
The multiple trills and screechings, different
From decibels in Italy or Provence:
Shrill carapace of shellac, trembling membranes
Strumming glum cacophonies.

And they are indeed alien, their quavers
Underline again
And yet again how different they, and we, are —
Like the nightingale that is not a nightingale,
The crow that will never be a crow,
Though sweet, though raucous.

And yet, in the swelter of summer, in a thick sweat,
Why not different?
They go with the twilight, the night, the day, the dawn
Coming again in shrill loudspeaker vans
Announcing news I cannot understand,
Speaking in tongues, wheezing out miracles.

Shock

An easing of walls,
A shuddering through soles:
A petal loosens, falls.

In the room, alone:
It begins, then it has gone.
Ripples outlast stone.

Rain-smell stirs the heart;
Nostrils flare. A breath. We wait
For something to start.

The flavour of fear,
Something fragile in the air.
Gone, it remains here.

Patterns

There is a word for the pattern in things –
The grain in bamboo, the markings in jade,
The lie of an animal's fur, strands in a thread.
Each has its quiddity of patternings,
And none can fade.

There is an order. There is a fixed place
Established within the pattern. The prince
Speaks only within his rank. It is a dance
Where each must put a mask before his face.
We must convince

The gruff barbarian that he cannot play
This skilful game, or even learn the rules:
Our scholars know his blundering reason fails
Trapped in the torments of the only Way
Taught in our schools.

They cannot penetrate our subtleties,
Our precepts of the Gods and of the shapes
Taken by the divinity that slips
Between us; between our divinities
And theirs – mere tropes,

Approximate translations, figures flicked
Inaccurately on a counting-frame.
Ours is a pattern flowing down a stream,
Not to be caught, a language none inflect
And none can tame.

Sideshows

at the Tori-no-Ichi

She is quite pretty, young, and she swallows fire.
Her kimono has a special bib to protect her.
She mops her mouth with tissues daintily
In preparation for the plume of flame.

After she has done the necessary – a conflagration
Sucked down her throat and belched with a roar upwards –
Our attention is drawn to a writhing sack of snakes.
She is handed one snake, which she smoothes like a length of string.

Then, with a steady hand, the snake's head is inserted
Between her lips; she inhales, and it disappears
Along with four inches of body. The drumming increases.
The body withdraws, headless. She frowns and chews,

Opens her mouth, allows a trickle of blood
To flow down her chin, and wipes it gently away.
She has swallowed the snake's head. She smiles at the joke.
She mops her mouth with tissues daintily.

⋆

She is three feet tall, her head and trunk are those
Of a woman of sixty; but her arms are short and muscled
Like an infant Hercules, and her legs are stumps
Wrapped in bright rags, taffeta sausages.

She plays with a saucer balanced on a stick
Which she twirls in time to the music. By her side
Is a life-sized head of a puppet. She puts her own head
On the floor, and raises her trunk with a flip of her wrists.

But something is wrong with the tape-recorder.
It should be giving her something to dance to,
With the puppet's head stuck in her crotch and her tiny stumps
Waving like arms though they are really legs.

An assistant is called for, a big young capable man
Who fiddles with switches and knobs. But the tape-recorder
Refuses to play the game. The crowd is waiting.
They have paid their money and are waiting for something to happen.

But nothing happens. Till the three-foot woman shrugs
With her massive shoulders, and begins to move,
Waving her ragged legs, jiggling the puppet's head
In time to nothing, in a silent dance.

Hiroshima: August 1985

No way to deal with it, no way at all.
We did not have to come, and yet we came.
The things we saw were all the very same
As we expected. We had seen them all:
The fabric pattern printed on the skin,
The shadow of a body on a wall.
What wrapped our bodies round was much too thin.

Voyeurs, but sensitive not to display
Unseemly horror; yet sensing that we felt
Horror was here, and everywhere was shown.
We knew the arguments the other way –
If they had had the thing, it would have blown
Some other city, one of ours, away.
Was it guilt, shame, fear, nausea that we smelt?

Self-accusations, bewilderment, disgust:
Those dripping rags of flesh, that faceless head,
The sky wiped black, the air crammed black with dust,
City of ghosts, museum of the dead.
No way to deal with it, no way at all.
We did not have to come, and yet we came.
The things we saw were all the very same
As we expected. We had seen them all.

On Dejima: 1845

A turn around the yard, then back again:
A pint of gin, a game of dice, to bed

Knocked out, locked in. Twenty-two exiled men
Marooned like ghosts who do not know they're dead.

Krieger talks rubbish. Blomhoff wants a whore
And says so, endlessly. Van Puyck adds up

Consignment figures for the umpteenth time.
Wail of a shakuhachi from the shore.

Tomorrow night, some fiefling in to sup:
Adam the cook prepares a fishy slime

Fit for outlandish palates, and sweet wine
To tilt his brains indulgently our way

('Your eminence, do take another cup') –
Turn a blind eye to Rahder's escapade

Last week (a scuffle on the landward side,
A bloody nose or two): we cover up

For one another like a gang of boys,
Distrust and honour shiftily in turn

Keeping the balance. Distantly, a noise
Of drum and cymbals marking out some rite

Pickled in superstition. Candles burn
Down to each dish, spit smoke, and then go out.

The hills of Nagasaki ring the night,
Our dark horizon where we cannot go.

Each day creeps by, each minute labours slow.
A hundred years from now, perhaps some light

Will fall upon this heathen harbour town –
But let the gin take over, let me row

My numbed, thick, sleepy body out to sea.
Let me go easy. Let me sink and drown

Far from this fan-shaped offshore prison where
Seabirds screech alien words in alien air.

Soseki

(London: December 1902)

A lost dog slinking through a pack of wolves.

Sour yellow droplets frozen on each branch.
The tainted breath of winter in the fog:
Coal-smells, and cooking-smells (meat-fat, stewed-fish),
And smells of horse-dung steaming in the streets:
Smoke groping at the windowpanes, a stain
Left hanging by the mean lamp where I trace
Page after page of Craig's distempered notes . . .

> Winter withering
> Autumn's last scattering leaves:
> London is falling.

I want a theory, a science with firm rules
Plotting the truth objectively through all these infinite spaces.
I look out of the window over the whitened blankness,
And from the East the moon lights up half the river.

But it is hallucination: cab-lights from Clapham Common
Flash at the pane, my head throbs over the little fire.
I am crying in the darkness, my cheeks sticky with tears.
Far, far beyond the heavens the forms of departing clouds . . .

Downstairs, those sisters plot and scheme together –
I found the penny on the windowsill,
The one I gave the beggar yesterday. Ridiculous pity.
Sly instruments of torture!
                              'Natsume's mad' –
That telegram sent home by Okakura –
Will they believe it? Is it so? Is he my friend?
I have no friends. By the light of the dying fire
I underscore these lines, and more, and more . . .

> December evening.
> Light at the window shining.
> Something in hiding.

London is districts learned from Baedeker
And learned on foot. England is somewhere else.
A day in Cambridge seeing Doctor Andrews,
The Dean of Pembroke, offering me sherry.
Too many 'gentlemen' – at Oxford too.
Someone said *Edinburgh*, but the speech up there
Is northern dialect, *Tohōku*-style.
So London it must be – the Tower, its walls
Scrawled with the dying words of men condemned:
Lodgings in Gower Street with Mrs Knot;
That vast Museum piled with pallid Greeks;
West Hampstead, and then Camberwell New Road . . .
I measure out the metres as I walk,
Finding sad poetry in the names of places.

Sometimes, walking the streets thronged with such tall and handsome
        ones,
I see a dwarf approaching, his face sweaty – and then
I know it for my own reflection, cast back from a shop-window.
I laugh, it laughs. 'Yellow races' – how appropriate.

'Least poor Chinese' – I think I hear – or 'Handsome Jap' . . .
Sneers of a group of labourers, seeing me go by
In frock-coat, top-hat, parody of 'English gentleman'
Sauntering down King's Parade or in the High . . .
I walk to Bloomsbury, walk back to Clapham,
Carry my Meredith or Carlyle through the drizzle,
Munching with difficulty a 'sandwich' on a bench in the park
Soaked by the rain, buffeted by the wind . . .

Far, far beyond the heavens the forms of departing clouds,
And in the wind the sound of falling leaves.

It is time to be deliberate, to use
Such gifts as I am given, to escape
The traveller's to-and-fro, the flow of facts
Unchecked, to make a system that will join
Blossom to branch, reason to intuition,
Wave after wave uniting as each falls
Under the next that follows up the beach . . .

A cry outside shakes
The tangle of waterpipes:
Midnight: a mouse squeaks.

A frightened mouse in a cell facing north,
I have almost forgotten what brought me here
Or what I do from day to day.
                                    I know
I sat with Craig for an hour this morning,
Hearing him mumbling Shakespeare through his beard,
Gave him my shillings in an envelope
Bound with ribbon which he plucked away
Impatiently and mannerless – due fee
For pedagogic drudgery. So walked back,
Wondering could I afford a mess of eggs
In the cabby-shelter out in Battersea,
And settled for a farthing bun and 'tea'
Scabby with milk served in a cracked white mug
At the stall by Wandsworth Bridge. Such humdrum things
To maze the mind and clog the intellect . . .

By the old castle at Komoro
The clouds are white and the wanderer grieves.

Impenetrable people, country bumpkins,
Nincompoop monkeys, good-for-nothing
Ashen-faced puppets – yes, it's natural
Westerners should despise us. They don't know
Japan, nor are they interested. Even if
We should deserve their knowledge and respect,
There would be neither – because they have no time
To know us, eyes to see us . . . Lesser breeds:
We need *improvement* (Brett has told me so),
And Western intermarriage would improve us.
We are the end of something, on the edge.

            The loneliness, the grieving heart of things,
            The emptiness, the solving fate that brings
            An answer to the question all men ask,
            Solution to the twister and the task.

94

'Tears welling up in a strange land,
I watch the sun set in the sea':
Yes, true, but for the sun, which once a week
May sidle itself weakly through pale clouds,
And for the sea, which somewhere – south or east –
Lies far beyond me, and is not my sea.
But tears well up, indeed, in a strange land
And speak of nothing but my lack of speech.
Curt monosyllables jab and jabber on,
Perverted versions of the tongue I know
Or thought I knew – the language Shakespeare spoke,
And Lemuel Gulliver's pure dictions mouthed
By me, alone, in Kanda, Matsuyama,
In Kumamoto . . . sailing through such seas
And on such seas of rhetoric and doubt
Towards these other islands where the sun
Has set before it rises, Ultima Thule,
Where tears well up and freeze on every branch.

I creep into my bed. I hear the wolves.

Great Foreign Writer Visits
Age-Old Temple,
Greeted by Venerable Abbess: 1955

GFW: I am most honoured
to be received here
this afternoon.

VA: We are very glad
that you came
despite the heat.

GFW: I hear there are
many National Treasures
in this temple.

VA: This building is itself
a National Treasure,
as is the Buddha
deified inside it.

GFW: May I ask
how old
the temple is?

VA: This temple
is one thousand four hundred
years old. I am the one hundred
and nineteenth abbess.

GFW: In what dynasty
was the temple founded?

VA: In the era
of the Emperor Kinmei,
when the Buddha came
to Japan . . . May I ask
your purpose in coming
to Japan?

GFW: I came to Japan
to know more about
the Japanese people
and Japanese culture,
of which we know something
in my country, and admire.

VA: And may I ask how long
you intend to stay?

GFW: Three weeks.

VA: In regard to religion,
are you studying Christianity
or Buddhism primarily?

GFW: I am interested in all religions
as a form of man's behaviour.

VA: Is this your first
visit to Japan?

GFW: Yes, but I have known
Japanese history
Japanese art
and Japanese literature
a long time.

VA: I feel very much assured
that you have so much understanding
towards these things.

GFW: Thank you very much.
I wish more people from my country
could know your people
and your country.

VA: Can you eat
this kind of
Japanese cake?

GFW:	I am sure I can because I like all Japanese food.
VA:	Are you giving a lecture or something?
GFW:	I am attending a seminar on our own country's literature.
VA:	It must be very trying in this hot season.
GFW:	No, this season is like the season at my home – very pleasant.
VA:	Have you a message for our youth? For the world? What is your impression of our women? Of God? May I ask what tobacco you smoke?
GFW:	To thine own self be true. May peace prevail. Very beautiful. The same to all but called by different names. A blend I have made up.
VA:	Thank you very much for coming.
GFW:	Thank you for all your trouble.
Together:	Thank you. Thank you. Thank you.
GFW:	*Arigato* . . . (Did I get that right?)

Imagine a City

Imagine a city. It is not a city you know.
You approach it either by river or by one of four roads,
Never by air. The river runs through the city.
The roads enter at the four points of the compass.
There are city walls, old ones, now long decayed
But they are still there, bits of a past it once had.

Approach it now (shall we say) by the road from the east.
You can see the ruined gate from a mile away,
And, beyond the gate, towers that may be temples or tombs.
It is evening, and smoke here and there is rising in drifts,
So meals are being prepared, you suppose, in thousands of houses.
There is a smell of roast meat, a succulent odour.

Now enter the city, go through the eastern gate.
Great birds, like vultures, shift on its broken tiles.
The street in front of you is obscured by the setting sun,
A yellow-red ball in a dazzling haze of brilliance.
The paving under your feet is uneven. You stumble,
Clutching a door that leans to your hand as you take it.

And now for the first time you are uneasy.
No one is in the street, or in the side-turnings,
Or leaning out from the windows, or standing in doorways.
The fading sunlight conspires with the drifting smoke,
Yet if there were people here surely you'd see them,
Or, at the least, hear them. But there is silence.

Yet you go on, if only because to go back now
Seems worse – worse (shall we say) than whatever
Might meet you ahead, as the street narrows, and alleys
Flow in hither and thither, a dead-end of tangles
Looping forwards and sideways, neither here nor there, but somehow
Changing direction like water wind-caught abruptly.

And there you are, now. You may find the western gate.
It must lie straight ahead, the north to your right,
The south to your left. But where is the river
You heard about (you say) at the beginning?
That is for you to find out, or not to find out.
It may not, in any case, serve as a way of escape.

You imagined a city. It is not a city you know.

The Dancing Foxes

An early morning walk in Gloucestershire
Twenty-five years ago: the borrowed cottage, then
A rutted track, a gate, a rising copse,
The wind blowing against me, when
Among the trees I reached another gate.

Leaning, at first I saw the distance rather
Than what the morning gave me . . . Straight
In front of me, six feet away, a vixen
Lay in a couch of bracken, muzzle raised
At her two cubs, dancing on their hind paws,
Rapt as their mother's gaze.
Nimbly they moved. Moved and unmoving, we
Watched as they danced, vixen and man content
In what we saw, separately and together.

Until the wind turned suddenly, to scatter
Vixen and cubs across those distances,
Leaving me at the gate among the trees.

The Return

I picked her up that hot sand-blasted day
In Euhesperides – a rubbish tip
Where all Benghazi's refuse piled across
Scatterings of a millennium of mess:
A broken head of earthenware, a face
Staring out silently, wreathed in her dress
Of fragile terracotta. Picked her up
And brought her home, and meant to let her stay.
She lodged there in a cabinet, and moved
As we moved, to this other place, and lay
For twenty years in England.
                  Till today
I looked inside the cabinet, observed
The spilth of dust and splinters at her neck,
A fallen garment. As I gently took
Her head within my hands, she split and broke,
Her chaplet and her vestiges of dress
Shivering to sand.
            I threw her all away
Onto the flowerbed: all of her except
The one remaining scrap, her oval face
Lying within my palm. I have it here,
This small masked relic. In this chilly year
The northern damps had killed her where she slept –

The last frail remnant of Persephone,
Whose head it was, whom I picked up that day
After so many broken centuries,
Miraculous and lasting testimony
Among the camel corpses, salt, tins, glass,
And brought her home to live here, till today
She went back to the underworld, as dust.

Her tiny face looks up, and will not last.

Multiplied

He's gone with her, and she has gone with him,
And two are left behind; and there's four more —
The children, two of each; grandparents, still
Alive and well, till now, and taking sides;
And neighbours, six close by, and more besides
In half a dozen villages . . . Until
The whole thing multiplies by seven score —
Why he went off with her, and she with him.

One, left behind, has changed the locks and keys:
The other keeps inside and draws the blinds.
The ones who went have rented somewhere near,
But no one's seen them yet. The children play
With neighbours' children. Those who've gone away
Will haggle over them, and fret in fear
Absence will blank them out. What clasps and binds
Shreds down to lawyers, judgements, mortgages.

So what began in two especial lives,
Involving many more in church and bank,
Florist, wine-merchant, dressmaker, Moss Bros.,
A regiment of relatives, a ring,
Has now become this other tangled thing:
Two grew to eight, with dozens at a loss
To know whom they should blame or love or thank.

So many husbands gone, so many wives.

Sigma

Unable to get on with anything,
Throwing out papers, fiddling with piled mess,
I pull a box of sherds out, stacked up here
Among the whole accumulation, less
Because I want to but because it's there –
A scattering of pottery I picked up
Among the Libyan middens I knew once,
And rake it over, chucking out here a cup-
handle, broken, and a flaking rim:
And, in among it all, there's suddenly
This scrap that carries a graffito – Σ,
A sigma, a scratched *ess*; and try to tell
Where it once fitted – as beginning or end,
As some abbreviated syllable,
Or sign of ownership, or just a scribble
Made on a day in 450 BC
By someone else who messed about like this,
Unable to get on with anything,
But made his mark for someone else to see.

Cockroach Story

'The reason for a cockroach in a story must differ from the reason for a cockroach in a kitchen.'

Leon Wieseltier, *TLS*

It was not home. It was in Tokyo
At half-past ten at night or thereabouts.
I went into the kitchen, flicked the switch,
And saw him crouching on the table's edge.

He was enormous, brown, and very still.
His feathery branches waited, so it seemed,
For further movement, and for me to move.
We looked at one another very hard.

He did not move, nor did I, watching him.
The jet-lag left me drowsy still, though sleep
Seemed far away, as I was far away.
I studied him as if in Japanese.

Aburamushi is the name for him
I suddenly remembered, wondering
What *abura* means: *mushi* is 'insect' or
A dozen other things in Japanese,

Such as a kind of soup, both clear and poached.
This cockroach, though, was more a samurai,
Plated and helmeted and plumed and proud.
I faced him as a common yokel might,

Lest he should shove me sideways with his sword,
Or leap across the tabletop and land
Bristling with fury in my sweating hair.
It was a hot September night, and I

Was tired of travel. 'I'll get it over with –
This stinker from the floorboards makes me sick,'
I thought, 'and I am sick of fantasy.'
I took one slipper off and lunged at him.

He skidded off the table, hit the floor
With a soft slushy plop, and sidestepped back
Towards the sink. I threw myself full-length
And smashed him with the slipper, and crouched down.

His scales fanned out. He bled onto the boards,
Gave half a shrug, and then lay still and dead.
I wiped the slipper with a newspaper,
Rinsed both my hands, and groped my way to bed.

That is the story. This is the poem, told
In metre, with a rhyme to end it all.
The reasons for the cockroach, or the poem,
Or why I've told the story – who can tell?

A cockroach in a kitchen is the truth.
A cockroach in a story may be lies.
The insect was both noble and uncouth.
The writer makes a life from mysteries.

Together, Apart

Too much together, or too much apart:
This is one problem of the human heart.

Thirty-five years of sharing day by day
With so much shared there is no need to say

So many things: we know instinctively
The common words of our proximity.

Not here, you're missed; now here, I need to get away,
To make some portion separate in the day.

And not belonging here, I feel content
When brooding on the portion that is spent.

Where everything is strange, and yet is known,
I sit under the trees and am alone,

Until there is an emptiness all round,
Missing your voice, the sweet habitual sound

Of our own language. I walk back to our room
Through the great park's descending evening gloom,

And find you there, after these hours apart,
Not having solved this question of the heart.

Potter

He took a lump of clay,
Squatted above his wheel,
Threw it a certain way,
Spun it till you could feel
His thumbs splay out the rim
And spin and spin and spin,
Then pulled, and pressed, and let
The clay become a jet
Rising, controlled by air,
Then let it go; and there,
Below the plume of clay,
Cut it and made it stay
Perfect, a moulded bowl.
Three more grew from the whole
Pillar of clay, and lay –
Accomplishments, and final.
      Till he took
These four perfections like a finished book
And closed the pages with his open hands,
Collapsing clay back into clay. His smile
Mocked at the skill he nullified, while
Only the shapeless lump remains and stands.

Interpreter

I am very nervous. You can tell I am very nervous.
The moment I greet you, I begin talking too much
And the words are not right, I know they are not right.
Anyway . . . They have asked me to do this job
Which means speaking your words in my words
And their words in your words, and so I begin
Talking too much before you have even begun
Using many words at all. In fact, as I say . . .
Anyway . . . I wish I could keep calm, and listen, and say
Exactly the words that they speak and you speak, and begin
To know what you want to know about what that is
Over there (I'm not sure – I think it historical).
Anyway . . . But now I begin to tell you about my life
Since you kindly asked a question, and so I go on –
Too much, too much – about father who passed away, and mother ill,
And how I was ill too, often, when young, and how
I never became married, because my fiancé
Disappeared – no, not exactly, he just stopped coming, and . . .
Anyway . . . That was a famous temple, I forget the name.
And I am a Latter Day Saint, which is very strange,
I know, in this country, but I know it is true for me,
And could be for you – but you are a Protestant,
Have I got the words right? And I have my faith, yes I do,
And though I am nervous I know it is true for me,
Though my colleagues despise me, and whisper about me, and are rude
In front of my face and behind my back, and I . . . Anyway . . .
Yes, I think we are stopping a moment to see this famous
Historical place, I forget the name, I don't know the words,
And believe me, believe me, believe me, dear foreign guest
(So kind in your questions, so gentle, so worried – I see)
You are welcome here, very welcome. Anyway . . .
Please excuse how nervous I am. I think I shall die.

Gairaigo*

Sitting in apāto
Quiet in my manshon
I write this in my nōto
Lacking a wāpuro.

I am on a tsuā
From faraway Yōroppa
Where I wear a toppā
Or ōbā in the winter.

Terebi and rajio
Speak to me Nihon-go.
Tabako, arukōru
Help my arubaito.

Invite me to a konpa,
Give me a haibōru,
I have no abekku . . .
Show me please the toiré.

Better fetch shaberu.
Now I need a beddo,
Feeling pretty ierō . . .
Ga-gi-gu-ge-go.

* Japanese 'words that come from outside'
apartment; mansion (block of flats); notebook; word-processor; tour; Europe; topcoat;
overcoat; television; radio; cigarettes; alcohol; work (from Ger. *arbeit*); party; highball;
girl-/boyfriend (from Fr. *avec*); toilet; shovel; bed; yellow.

Recreational Leave

They have come back. The next lot is in,
Landing at the port. Soon they will be here,
Some a little bit drunk, some a lot drunk,
With their money, their condoms, their loud pink faces.

They will be here soon. I tidy up the place,
Making the mattress nice, hanging the curtain
Just in the right place, bringing the water
So they can have a wash before it begins.

And afterwards too: they like to have a good wash
Before and after. I put out a tray with two cups,
Which some of them will fill with whisky or beer
And some of them will not. I want to make them happy.

Some of them are happy already, but I hope not too happy.
I don't want a lot of noise, or slapped faces,
With my baby here close by under the netting.
On a good night, I can have maybe ten of them in

With their money, their condoms, their loud pink faces,
And no trouble at all, if they are not too happy
With whisky or beer or whatever they want to do
To show they are proper men and enjoying themselves.

Nobody wants any trouble. Anyway, I don't.
If they are happy, and pay, and go away,
I shall be happy. My aunt will be happy too.
I put on my good dress, and wait for the sound

Of their funny voices banging about outside,
And try to guess what sort of a night it will be.
Baby, be quiet, I am here. I am fifteen.
This is the way I live, on the edge of the port.

Final Verdict Tours

Having crossed the ultimate checkpoint to our friendly nation,
You have twenty minutes to see this ancient city.
There is the Black Fort and the Basalt Church,
The Basilica of Unrighteousness, the Mosque of Envy,
The Lukewarm Baths, and the successive quarters
Inhabited by the Extremish, the Waverish, the Vilipends.

Behold the monuments to antique unfortunates:
The sad exit of Hadad the Excitable
Torn to pieces in a popular uprising,
The sublime martyrdom of Rashap the Vulgar
Subdued by applied arachnids under the armpits.
We are proud of our heritage among such enactments.

Observe our more recent manifestations of culture –
The picturesque garments of the tolerated minorities,
The gorgeous pictography of the eliminated tribes.
(Avoid the offered sherds, the reproductions:
You may be seduced by cunning artifices
Replicated in the bazaars and in humble courtyards.)

Here are the products of the curious contemporary,
Desirable to those with an eye for excellence:
Embroideries by hand, paintings by foot
Achieved by those whose hands have been excised
For various offences considered capital
But for the amnesty of our President and his mercies.

We allow for a rest-stop at the end of such plenitude –
A packed lunch available, the spirits extra:
Any currency is valid, though temptingly fluctuating.
Then back to the bus, please, in orderly fashion.
Tonight at Happy Hour the evening's rubric.
Tomorrow our departure for the last resort.

Gone

Down in the dark water
Where the quick mill-race flows,
Something hidden rises,
Something secret goes.

Rising, it flashes whitely.
Going, it sinks below.
You cannot recognise it.
You see the water flow

Quickly under the mill-race,
Race down and reach the pond.
Whatever you have seen there
Goes on and out, beyond

Your vision or your knowledge,
Untethered to one place.
It glints, and hints, and teases,
And shows you your own face

Peering below the sluice-gate,
Watching the mill-race fall
Forever and forever,
With not a word at all

Of what you saw — or fancied
You saw — rise up and sink
One moment in the water,
The next over the brink.

Memoir

He writes what he remembers, innocent,
Though now he is no longer innocent:
What he remembers, what he tries to write,
Is how things were. He cannot get it right.

The words go down on paper. In between
Another sheet of paper lies between
The sheet he writes on and the page beneath.
Something is lying down there, underneath.

And it is those words, on the page below,
That somehow stick, as he goes down below
Experience to innocence, and finds
The thing he looked for is the thing he finds.

But in the morning, reading what he wrote
Last night, the only words he finds he wrote
Are on the surface. And the page below
Is blank as things he did not want to know.

For George MacBeth

Wasted away –
Limbs, speech, and breath –
Such mockery, such sprightly gay
Spirits smothered, friend
Stubborn to call it death.
Make it all end.

Last words are right:
You whispered them
That last intolerable night,
Darkness itself, deep
Gathering of choked phlegm –
'How long will I sleep?'

September 3rd 1939: Bournemouth

My summer ends, and term begins next week.
Why am I here in Bournemouth, with my aunt
And 'Uncle Bill', who something tells me can't
Be really my uncle? People speak
In hushed, excited tones. Down on the beach
An aeroplane comes in low over the sea
And there's a scattering as people reach
For towels and picnic gear and books, and flee
Towards the esplanade. Back at the hotel
We hear what the Prime Minister has said.
'So it's begun.' 'Yes, it was bound to.' 'Well,
Give it till Christmas.' Later, tucked in bed,
I hear the safe sea roll and wipe away
The castles I had built in sand that day.

Evacuation: 1940

Liverpool docks. The big ship looms above
Dark sheds and quays, its haughty funnels bright
With paint and sunlight, as slim sailors shove
About with chains and hawsers. Mummy's hand
Is sticky in my own, but I'm all right,
Beginning an adventure. So I stand
On a deck piled high with prams, the staterooms shrill
With mothers' mutterings and clasped babies' cries.
I squirm and tug, ten years impatient, till
Loud hootings signal something . . . The surprise
Of hugging her, feeling her face all wet:
'Mummy, you're sweating.' They were tears; not mine.
She went away. I was alone, and fine.

Pleasure, and guilt. Things you do not forget.

Maturity: 1944

A son, fourteen, home to father and mother
After four years away. The one who went
A child, this one returning as a man
Almost: his voice broken, speaking American.
He was their son, but somehow now another:
The years of absence forced them to invent
New habits for this foreigner.
                                            So then
The father, fooling about, faced up to the boy,
Put up his fists: they could behave like men
In manly parody. And the son, to join in the game,
Put his up too, pretending they were the same,
And struck. The father's nose gushed out with blood.
The son watched, appalled. And never understood
Why his father leapt, and cried, and cried with joy.

Snakes (Virginia, 1940)

Down in the creek, snakes:
Snakes in the opposite wood.
There were snakes everywhere.
This was new. This was good.

At home in England, snakes
Were pets in a glass cage.
Here they slipped free, and swam.
This was a golden age.

Most folk I knew hated snakes,
Shrank if I brought one back
And let it run over my arm
Or gathered and then lay slack.

Whipsnakes, cornsnakes, snakes
Swollen, and black, and green,
Crept through my days and nights.
This was the primal scene.

And there were other snakes,
Ones to be cautious of:
Cottonmouths, copperheads, once
A rattler I saw in a grove.

How to account for these snakes
In a boy uprooted at ten
In a war that spanned a world
He would not see again?

Eden did not have snakes:
Only one snake, it is said.
We know what that single snake
Did. Or so we have read.

I had not read it then.
All I knew was I loved the things.
Years on, I call them all back,
Sinuous rememberings.

Philip Larkin in New Orleans

Suppose he had come here, two days after Mardi Gras,
The wrong time. It would be raining
In sheets up from the Delta, the banquettes awash
And the gutters running with all the festival trash:
Laughing-gas capsules, confetti, a tinsel star,
Cheap beads, purple and golden and green,
Bottle-caps, condoms, masks. Somewhere too far,
Somewhere too foreign. He would be complaining
This wasn't the dream he had had, the dream-place he'd been —
Tapping his feet in a bar in Bourbon or Basin, the moan
Of riverboats drifting through the Vieux Carré
Mingling with a familiar saxophone,
And the girls stepping out on the streets at the end of the day.

His Crescent City is much further off,
A paradise where love and trumpets play
In tune, and out of time, beyond belief
In ordinary days or usual grief,
A place in which all doubt is put away.
Tonight I caught his authentic other note,
Fixed, finite, steady in its monotone,
As I passed an old black with a graveyard cough,
An empty bottle, a funereal hat,
Who muttered something as he cleared his throat,
Trembled, and batted off the rain, and spat
Somewhere between Decatur and Wilk Row,
His hopes expelled with an enormous no.

NEW POEMS

Deus Absconditus

In every temple compound, under some tree
Exhausted by its effort to grow
Unwatered, yet festooned in faded silks,
These bits of broken holiness abound:
Stone, plaster, plastic, terracotta, wood,
Carved, moulded, fired, gaudy with crimson and gold,
The head or the feet of the Buddha, a smashed plaque,
A dancing acolyte dismembered, strewn
Together with green sherds of splintered glass,
Spirals of dog-turds, spills of litter, muck
Preserving all this shattered deity.

One in particular I coveted –
A headless ivory figurine, its arms
Spread out in blessing, each tiny fold of robe
Distinctly beautiful, and intricate,
And perfect in its three-inch skilfulness.
Discarded, not destroyed; not thrown away;
Not quite abandoned . . . No one would know, I knew,
And yet I knew I could not pocket it,
Assembled, humbled, among all that trash.
Lust for possession stunted me, a tree
Knowing there might be life there, somewhere, still.

Coming Back from Kawau

Coming back from Kawau, on the last ferry,
We passed them on the way: a smaller island
From which projected a small jetty
And on the jetty half-a-dozen, waving.

We hadn't seen them on the way there, coming
Early in the brilliant day, the sun
Glaring across the bay, our concentration
Fixed on Grey's miniature Victorian mansion –

A white colonial outpost among ferns,
Composed and elegant, the edge of empire
Preserved in its own tidiness, remains
Unpeopled among urns and furniture.

I saw its set perfection, its apartness,
Its faded photographs, proconsular
Relics of duty, its still orderliness,
Remote and separate as a distant star.

Yet coming back, those valedictory waves
Came back more strongly, strangely, as we passed
Too far to hear them, or to see them clearly,
Like an experience, somehow, we had missed.

They dipped into the distance, and were gone,
And ours, the day's last ferry, journeyed on.

Changing Ties

Changing my tie in the lavatory
From black to flowery,
In the train from the funeral
Travelling south to the wedding,
Having said farewell
To the dead and preparing a greeting
To those about to be married –

In the same dark suit appropriate to either
One or the other,
Only the fancy tie is different,
A quick metamorphosis
Scarcely planned or meant:
Leaving what was, moving towards what is,
The past, the present, the living, the dead.

Snake in Autumn

A lithe fat flash of light below the compost
Reveals his coils, flesh swollen, slowly writhing
In warm October leaves. One eye is blind.
A wound along his body weeps with pus.
I pick him up and cradle his old age,
His sightless eye, his unhealed stinking gash,
Study his proud exhaustion, his sad fear,
Then gently put him down. He slithers off
Back into barricades of compost, back
Into the winter of death, and out of sight.

Trebonianus Gallus

My father's joke – *Trebonianus Gallus* –
An obscure emperor's name, that made me shout
And jump about and go for him . . . How this
Ritual was endorsed, or how the joke began,
I do not know, I can't remember. Eight,
Perhaps I was, or even younger, when
This private bit of nonsense started. It
Must have been something shared through Roman coins,
Fingering all those scraps of well-rubbed bronze
Bought with my pocket-money: tray on tray,
And Seaby's catalogue spread out between us,
Puzzling, identifying. *Trebonianus Gallus* –
I had forgotten him, until today
The name, your impish face, our childish game,
Sixty years later broke into my head,
Hearing my grandson tease me with the same
Complicitous sharing, as I threw a name
Towards him, knowing you there, and dead.

Passing On

Simon, my grandfather, born in '72,
Told me the tale of how, as a young boy
He stood in Bradford City Hall and saw
The high-winged collar Gladstone wore wilt low.

The great man spoke for hours. The sweat poured down.
Nothing he said could Grandad quite recall.
Tonight, in '96, I pass this on
To my own grandson. But I cannot tell

Whether, a hundred years from now, his own
Grandson will tell this thing that once was said
About the sweating high-winged orator, one
Who spoke across two centuries, unheard.

Object Lessons

I

'But there's no index', I said, turning the pages.
'Ah, yes', he said. 'And you're not the first
To comment on that. But we wanted to give more space
To the stuff itself, which is what most people want'.

The stuff itself flicked under my fingers,
Lots of it, moving at speed, till it seemed
Like those fat little joke-books I had as a child:
A cartoon animated by the turning pages.

Then I got to the end, and no index. Then
I made my comment, and he responded.
It seemed the end of the conversation.
A blur of pages, with no index at the end.

II

Because it was damaged, he said, he would bring down the price.
I couldn't see any damage, but I kept quiet,
Not wanting to show I'd not noticed. With a set face
I turned it round in my hand, and thought it all right.

He brought down the price, and I bought it. And now and again
I fetch the pot down from the shelf and examine it all
In the palm of my hand, never finding the flaw or the mend
That made me buy it at the price at which he would sell.

III

I found it on a market-stall in Skopje,
Not knowing what it was: bright tapestry,
Orange and red. It was a mystery.
My mother made it into a tea-cosy.

Now, when I'm pouring out a cup of tea
From this transmogrified fragility,
I sometimes face a visitor with a query:
'What do you think this curious thing might be?'

It seems it was, at least originally,
A decoration for a trousered knee
Worn by some Macedonian. But could it really be
A relic of the sole one-legged evzone in Skopje?

Elegiac Stanzas

The famous poet's mistress, forty years ago,
Now heard five times a week on radio
Acting an ageing upper-class virago.

'The deadbeats of the Caves de France, the suicidal',
The substance of a novelist's rapt recall,
One who escaped the death from alcohol.

The ravaged visage of a copywriter
Who was an intimate of him and her,
Encountered at the funeral of another.

And at memorial services the pews
Filling with this and that long-unseen face,
This one thought dead, that one no longer news.

And, rooting among boxes in the attic,
Letters another wrote, witty, ecstatic,
Who dwindled down to paperback-roundup critic.

And in the obit. columns an old queen
Wheeled on weekly recalling the has-been
Who've died in Tokyo, Paris, Golders Green.

These are the days of death, *memento mori*:
'I knew him as an undergraduate, before he . . . '
Turned into nothingness, the old old story.

These are the daily shades, the presences
Among the shadows, pricking the five senses
As they reveal themselves as absences.

These are the scourers, enemies of promise,
Rubbing out vanity and fame like pumice,
Asking to see the evidence like Thomas.

The famous poet's mistress, forty years ago,
And boxes crammed above, pews full below.
These are the things we hear, and see, and know.

Education

It used to be learning things over and over again
In a drone round the room repeating the things that were said:
The names of the countries, the names of the famous dead,
The multiplication tables, the figures for sun and rain
On the countries, the dates of the battles won
And the battles lost, the different spellings of words
Sounding the same, and – to make it a bit more fun –
The names of the butterflies, moths, mammals, fish, birds.

And now it is making up shapes and colouring each
For something called Projects, and making up other stuff
For something called Poetry, which no one wants to teach
Because it has rules and no one knows enough
To know how the rules work, and no one can hear
Because of the noise all round and the weight of the stuff
Out there in the world, full of names, dates, figures, fear.

The Property of the Executors

i.m. G.F.H.

It might have been a wedding, or a wake,
Some sort of celebration, a solemnity:
Or is it just shopping for shopping's sake,
A ritual cupidity?
Arriving through the morning mist, the cars
Inclined these visitors
Towards the great dead house now stripped, the striped marquee
Smothering with canvas and plastic the long lawns
He had kept in order, until his will bent,
And he put the gun to his head, and the whole thing went
Down to this one event.

My neighbour yawns
After four hours of this, the auctioneer
Jollying along each lot by lot by lot.
Yes, I agree with her, it's much too hot,
And my other neighbour reaches below his chair
For a swig at his beer, and the objects are raised in the air
By acolytes who respond to the numbers called
By the man who calls out money-names without fear
Of interruptions because, however appalled
Some of us are at this show,
This is the way such rituals must go.

The tables, the chairs, the mirrors, the carved blackamoor,
Then the pictures ('After' whoever and all),
The big mahogany chest that stood in the hall
Along with the cracked Staffordshire, the pattern fish slice,
The wrought-iron door-stop against the front door,
Silver, and screens, and glass.
All of them have their value, most of them fetch their price.

Then the books are parcelled out. Some singles, some pairs,
Some 'Miscellaneous. Quantity'. Here
Is one signed by all of the children for Mama, then *Paradise
Lost*, red morocco, Victorian, all
Jumbled up as home used to be, some below stairs,
Some elevated like trophies, things you could call

Treasures. But the auctioneer
Hurries on to the 'General Contents', the job lots,
At the end of a long hot day.

I stay, anyway,
To Lot Seven-Eleven, 'A Collection
Of Power and Hand tools, etc.', to see who may
Make a bid for it. But when it comes, late on,
The lot is split: Seven-Eleven A
Is what I look for, now described 'As Is':
A leather gun-case, initialled on its lid;
Inside, its wooden rods, its brass accoutrements,
Its roll of cotton pull-through; but the space
In which the shotgun should have been, not hid
But glaring open, empty, like the face
Of someone who should have been there. No offence
Intended. An emptiness instead.

Lot Seven-Forty goes. That is the end.
Loud quacking county voices void the tent
Bent on returning home to Cley and Wells.
I grope through autumn twilight, smell the smells
Of furnace-wood cut by a man now dead
Whose stuff this was, who maybe never meant
To cause all this, this sale, this wake, but can't transcend
What he has brought about. Whatever he meant.

Bibliographical note

The poems in this selection originally appeared in the following volumes:

Home Truths, Marvell Press, 1957
'Death of a Rat', 'To My Unborn Child'

The Owl in the Tree, Oxford University Press, 1963
'Mr Cooper', 'Night Thoughts', 'At Birth', 'White Snow', 'Hedgehog'

The Stones of Emptiness, Oxford University Press, 1967
'At Dunwich', 'Lesson', 'Dust', 'Buzzards Above Cyrene', 'Arabic Script', 'Ali Ben Shufti', 'The Letters of Synesius' I–XII

Inscriptions, Oxford University Press, 1973
'Monologue in the Valley of the Kings', 'At the Frontier Post: Om', 'Soldiers Plundering a Village', 'Worm Within', 'The Bonfire', 'Entry', 'Elsewhere', 'Inscriptions', 'Points'

A Portion for Foxes, Oxford University Press, 1977
'The Procession', 'By the Sluice', 'At the Indus', 'Thomas', 'Rescue Dig', 'A Portion for Foxes', 'Marriages', 'Simple Poem', 'Essays in Criticism', 'A Girdle Round the Earth', 'For Louis MacNeice', 'Called For'

Victorian Voices, Oxford University Press, 1980
'At Marychurch', 'Messages from Government House', 'After High Table', 'A Message from Her', 'From the Villa Massoni'

Letter from Tokyo, Hutchinson, 1987
'Letter from Tokyo', 'Cicadas in Japan', 'Shock', 'Patterns', 'Sideshows', 'Hiroshima: August 1985', 'On Dejima: 1845', 'Soseki', 'Great Foreign Writer . . .', 'Imagine a City', 'The Dancing Foxes'

Poems 1953–1988, Hutchinson, 1989
'The Return', 'Multiplied', 'Sigma'

The Dust of the World, Sinclair-Stevenson, 1994
'Cockroach Story', 'Together, Apart', 'Potter', 'Interpreter', 'Gairaigo', 'Recreational Leave', 'Final Verdict Tours', 'Gone', 'Memoir', 'For George MacBeth', 'September 3rd 1939: Bournemouth', 'Maturity: 1944', 'Snakes (Virginia, 1940)', 'Philip Larkin in New Orleans'

(New Poems)

Acknowledgements are due to the editors of the following publications, in which some of these uncollected poems have appeared:

Spectator ('Deus Absconditus', 'Snake in Autumn', 'The Property of the Executors')

London Magazine ('Coming Back from Kawau', 'Changing Times', 'Trebonianus Gallus', 'Passing On')

New Writing 6, Vintage, 1997 ('Object Lessons')

London Review of Books ('Elegiac Stanzas')